Raising Twice-Exceptional Children

Just because a child is gifted doesn't mean they don't have other types of neurodivergence, like ADHD, autism, dyslexia, and more. Conversely, even children with one of these diagnoses can be cognitively gifted. *Raising Twice-Exceptional Children* provides you with a road map to understand the complex make-up of your "gifted-plus," or twice-exceptional, child or teen.

The book helps you understand your child's diagnosis, meet their social-emotional needs, build self-regulation skills and goal setting, and teach self-advocacy. It also shows you effective ways to collaborate with teachers and school staff, and it offers advice on finding strengths-based strategies that support development at home.

For too long, these kids have fallen through the cracks. This book provides key information on how to best support neurodivergent children by leveraging their strengths while supporting their struggles.

Emily Kircher-Morris, LPC, is a mental health counselor for gifted and twice-exceptional people and host of *The Neurodiversity Podcast*. Growing up as a twice-exceptional kid led her to pursue supporting neurodivergent kids for her career. She has two identified twice-exceptional kids, and her youngest is still to be determined.

Raising
Twice-Exceptional
Children

A Handbook for Parents of
Neurodivergent Gifted Kids

Emily Kircher-Morris

Routledge
Taylor & Francis Group

NEW YORK AND LONDON

Cover image: Shutterstock

First published 2022
by Routledge
605 Third Avenue, New York, NY 10158

and by Routledge
2 Park Square, Milton Park, Abingdon, Oxon, OX14 4RN

Routledge is an imprint of the Taylor & Francis Group, an informa business

Library of Congress Cataloging-in-Publication Data
A catalog record for this book has been requested

ISBN: 978-1-646-32214-5 (pbk)
ISBN: 978-1-003-23753-2 (ebk)

DOI: 10.4324/9781003237532

Typeset in Palatino
by Apex CoVantage, LLC

For Grayson, Maggie, and Trevor
who taught me more about parenting than any degree,
expert, or book ever could

For Dave
my partner on this neurodivergent parenting journey

Contents

Acknowledgments

I'm grateful for the people I've met whose path I crossed or whose journeys aligned with mine for some time. There are too many to mention, but your influence has helped me to reach this life, which I wouldn't change for anything.

Thank you to my clients and their families, whose openness, vulnerability, and growth have shown me the beauty of neurodiversity. You've taught me about the strength of listening and the gradual process of healing.

Paula Williams, Dora Angevine, Erin Burke, Colleen Chiapel, Beth Cieslak, Madeline Kaleel, Heather Kuehnl, Pam Lueders, and Stefanie O'Neill at Unlimited Potential Counseling & Education Center: You've built an amazing neurodiversity-affirming practice and picked up my slack when I'm burning the candle at both ends. Thank you for being a part of this vision.

Thanks to the editors and staff at both Prufrock Publishing and Routledge Taylor & Francis Group for your consistent support and guidance throughout the process of creating this book.

And finally, a debt of gratitude is owed to my family, especially: Pauline Gouvin and Allen Kircher for supporting all of my endeavors and ideas over the years; Grayson, Maggie, and Trevor for being the most amazing, funny, loving kids they are; and Dave Morris, for being my podcast producer and parenting partner, and who loves me more than I probably deserve. (PS Dave – I'm sorry this isn't a book about dolphins.)

Introduction

Every day, I sit with my clients and their parents in the therapy room. My clients are mostly neurodivergent kids and teens and their parents. I feel comfortable listening to them share their story and help them feel comfortable with it, too. We brainstorm ideas together to help overcome executive functioning difficulties or to improve communication within the family or with peers. We strategize about accommodations that may be effective at home or in the classroom. We celebrate the successes and find the opportunities within the struggles, embracing the slow, plodding work of therapy.

Then I go home to my own family. We are a mostly happy constellation of twice-exceptional folks all living under one roof. And I want you to know that, just like you, I'm doing the best I can, minute by minute, with whatever reservoir of patience I can muster.

I'm sure you've heard someone joke, "If only kids came with a manual!" Of course, they don't. And even if they did, a lot of what was in it wouldn't be applicable to our twice-exceptional kids. This book, also, is not a manual. In the business world, a manual provides the exact procedures to complete a specific task, one by one, in order to achieve a certain outcome; I can't provide you with a manual for your child because that is something you and your child need to create that is unique to their own needs.

DOI: 10.4324/9781003237532-1

What I *can* provide is a handbook. A handbook is a framework for developing the procedures that work best for you.

In business, handbooks also align with a mission. The mission of this book is *to provide people raising twice-exceptional youth with the tools to create a neurodiversity-affirming environment for their families.* Everything within this book aligns with this mission, whether it is talking to your child about their diagnoses, advocating for them in the educational setting, or building the lifelong skills that will help neurodivergent people find success.

For years, my profile picture on social media has been a picture of a white coffee cup with the words "World's Okayest Mom" broadly written across it. I love this reminder that raising kids isn't a contest, that nobody is perfect, and that I am a good enough parent. I promise that I am far from perfect. Parenting twice-exceptional kids means we were thrown into the deep end of parenting without knowing exactly how deep it was.

I've had people refer to me as an expert and I always cringe at the word. (Once someone referred to me as an influencer. That just made me laugh!) I don't consider myself an expert: I can't be an expert on anyone else's child. *You* are the expert. You're the one who has had the experiences that brought you to this place and you are the one who knows your child. I promise you: I don't have all the answers. What I can do is help you brainstorm ideas to help you find the answers that can work for you and your family.

Being a twice-exceptional adult has set me up quite well to write this book. As a gifted/ADHDer, I have had a range of career experiences to draw from. (ADHD adults frequently change jobs.) I started my career as an elementary classroom teacher and then earned a master's degree in education with certification in gifted education. I spent almost ten years as a gifted education facilitator at the elementary and middle school levels. While I was teaching, I went back to school again and earned a second master's degree in school and professional counseling. I worked for a few years as a school counselor while building my private practice where I now provide mental health counseling services to gifted and twice-exceptional people. In 2018, my husband and I started *The Neurodiversity Podcast* (formerly

Mind Matters) where we share interviews with experts on topics related to the development of neurodivergent folks. Oh, and we have three neurodivergent children who, at the time of writing, are 13, 11, and 6.

Next-Level Parenting

Raising twice-exceptional kids is definitely next-level parenting … and there are no tutorials or easy levels to start. We are living in a society that doesn't understand the needs of giftedness or disability, and here we are, trying to navigate both! As we launch into our journey of helping you understand and support your neurodiverse family, there are a few aspects of parenting that I'd like you to keep in mind.

Positive Parenting
As a humanistic therapist, I use the framework of positive psychology with my clients. We work together to focus on the strengths that already exist and foster those. I don't let my clients beat themselves up when they make a mistake; we examine the situation without judgment and make plans to change how similar situations play out the next time.

Positive psychology also operates from the belief that people are more likely to be drawn toward goals in the future, rather than driven by past mistakes. This forward motion is key when we are utilizing strengths-based interventions. Neurodiversity-affirming practices are inherently strengths-based and driven from positive psychology beliefs.

As parents of neurodivergent children and teens, we are going to translate the positive psychology movement into our parenting practice. We're going to focus on resilience and leveraging the abilities our children innately have. Our children are different and quirky and receive negative messages from the world on a daily basis about how they don't quite fit. We are going to push back against this narrative and help our children value both their strengths and struggles and recognize how their unique combination of skills is what makes them who they are. We're working to help them grow into independent adults who advocate for themselves and aren't ashamed of being neurodivergent.

Our relationship with our children is the foundation to this work. There is a natural ebb and flow of growth and stagnation as children develop. Neurodivergent kids' development is asynchronous, and that is just fine. As parents implementing a positive psychology framework with our twice-exceptional kids, we know our work will help our children reach their finish line – it just might not be on the timeline we expected.

Where Are We Headed?

There is a therapeutic intervention that all counseling trainees learn in the early days of their program. It is called using the "Miracle Question." A therapist asks this question to a client framed in this way: "If you woke up tomorrow, and some miracle had happened overnight which solved the problem you came here for, what would be different that would let you know the problem had been solved?" This helps the client to crystallize what the problem is and drives the direction of the counseling sessions.

So, I'm going to ask you the same question: If after reading this book, you woke up and the problem that brought you to this book in the first place were solved, how would you know the problem had been solved? What would look different in your world and your daily life that would show you it had been solved? Think about it for a second.

Perhaps your answer is something along these lines:

◆ I would feel more confident as a parent and would spend less time feeling worried and anxious about making the right or wrong decisions.
◆ I wouldn't panic at parent–teacher conference time because I'd know my son or daughter is receiving appropriate educational challenge and support.
◆ Our family would be more harmonious. My child and I would be better able to communicate with each other because we are both more aware of their needs.

- ◆ Homework time wouldn't be a crisis every night because my child had built self-regulating skills to help their behavior and motivation.
- ◆ My child wouldn't hate going to school every day because they feel comfortable enough to advocate for their needs in the classroom.

What is the big picture vision that you are hoping to accomplish? What small steps can you identify that will help you reach that vision? Take some time to clarify this idea and consider specifically what changes would be evidence that change has occurred. That's where we're headed.

Progress, Not Perfection

As we embark on this journey, just a quick reminder that there aren't any quick fixes. Neurodiversity is based in brain wiring, and the difficulties that our children have aren't just bad habits or defiance. We are able to build compensatory strategies – and twice-exceptional folks have lots of strengths to pull from – but it is okay if the first thing you try doesn't work. It's also okay if you try something and it works for a while and then seems like it stops working. This is all totally normal.

A quick example: Let's say you are working on developing executive functioning skills for your son or daughter. Together, you might manage the executive functioning deficits they are facing currently, but as they get older, the expectations for executive functioning skills continue to grow. There may continue to be a lag in maturity and skills, requiring accommodations or support.

In these situations, don't lose hope and don't give up! Progress is gradual, and just because one goal was reached doesn't mean that subsequent goals will come automatically. But, you'll be able to step away, little by little, until your child is able to manage most things independently – or ask for help when they need it. And *that* is the success we're seeking.

What Do *You* Need?

I'm not a big fan of the term "self-care." I feel like it has been commercialized to the point that people think it means taking a soak in a jacuzzi while on vacation, eating bonbons, and drinking red wine. Self-care is much broader than that, and generally much more boring (although at least less expensive).

A component of self-care that I feel goes often unrecognized is self-compassion. Compassion involves acts of support driven by empathy. Self-compassion requires understanding our emotions, giving ourselves permission to be imperfect, and forgiving ourselves for the mistakes we feel we've made. As we navigate the world of parenting twice-exceptional kids, we're going to make mistakes. We're going to project our emotions about our own past onto our kids. And there's a good chance that, at some point in time, you will feel like you haven't done enough, or you've done too much, or whatever you did, you did it wrong.

Hand-in-hand with self-compassion is self-acceptance. Self-acceptance – recognizing our own strengths and struggles without judgment – is another key to having self-compassion. "Acceptance" in this situation doesn't mean resignation to helplessness; it means knowing that some things come more easily than others and we need to build the support around ourselves to accommodate for them.

Why are self-compassion and self-acceptance such integral components of supporting your child? There are several reasons. Chances are, if you are raising a neurodivergent child, you may be neurodivergent yourself. As parents, we are constantly in a fluctuating relationship with our children. We see ourselves in their behaviors and their words, simultaneously looking into a mirror of our past selves and trying to steer them, knowing what is only a bit further down the path.

If you are a person who is constantly berating yourself for poor executive functioning skills, how will that come across to your child? Do they hear or see you engaging in negative self-talk? Do you project that emotion onto them when you are trying to coach them? If you struggled with dyscalculia or dyslexia as a child and feel shame surrounding your academic history, will that emotion seep into your interactions with your child? How will your self-beliefs influence your relationship with your child? Or do you blame yourself for your child's difficulties, thinking of yourself as a bad parent?

Self-acceptance and self-compassion are necessary to support your child. We all make mistakes. We all have some things we're really good at and some things that could use some improvement. Each of us has parenting moments that weren't examples of our best selves. And each of us can strive to do better while holding space for self-acceptance and self-compassion.

By engaging in these practices, you are also going to teach your child to live in a space with self-acceptance and self-compassion. These building blocks provide the confidence necessary to ask for help and create the accommodations that many twice-exceptional people need throughout their lives.

How to Use This Book

This book is sorted into four major sections. Whether you are a read-straight-through or a skip-around-and-find-what-works type of reader, you are welcome to do either.

Part I of the book is all about understanding neurodiversity, giftedness, and twice-exceptionality. Chapter 1 explores the history of neurodiversity and how the neurodiversity movement is changing the way we view divergent people. Chapter 2 focuses on understanding the "typical (atypical)" development of twice-exceptional learners within the context of their giftedness. Chapter 3 dives into the many diagnoses that might be combined with giftedness to create a twice-exceptional profile, including considerations of how giftedness might play into how these diagnoses manifest. Also included in this chapter is information about seeking an assessment for diagnosis.

Part II of the book includes a parents' toolkit of strategies for you to consider as you support your twice-exceptional child. Each of the topics addressed in the parent toolkit section of the book will help you to implement the strategies included in Part III. Chapter 4 discusses how to talk to your child about twice-exceptionality. Chapter 5 looks at ways to communicate with your twice-exceptional child that encourage connection (especially for neurodivergent kids who may have different styles of communicating). Chapter 6 considers the issues related to co-parenting a twice-exceptional child with your partner.

Part III includes five chapters, each dedicated to the skills that all twice-exceptional kids need. We talk about why these skills are so important for our twice-exceptional children and how you can help to coach your child to build these skills from a strengths-based approach. The five skills that I've found that twice-exceptional kids struggle with and need are self-advocacy (Chapter 7), emotional regulation (Chapter 8), executive functioning (Chapter 9), effective communication within social relationships (Chapter 10), and self-directed motivation (Chapter 11).

Finally, the book wraps up with information about how to understand school options for your twice-exceptional child. Part IV includes two chapters: Chapter 12 examines the various types of school settings and programs to determine what might be available and appropriate for your twice-exceptional child, and Chapter 13 provides ideas and suggestions for effectively collaborating with school personnel.

Twice-exceptional children are unique and have amazing abilities that deserve to be nurtured and supported. I hope this book will provide an opportunity for you to gain a greater understanding of your twice-exceptional child and ideas for how to support them as they grow into the amazing people they are meant to be.

Let's get started!

PART

I

Understanding Neurodiversity, Giftedness, and Twice-Exceptionality

Understanding the framework of neurodiversity and how our conception of neurodiversity has changed is foundational to the types of supports that twice-exceptional children need. Throughout Part I of this book, we'll discuss the history of neurodiversity and how creating a neurodiversity-affirming environment for our kids benefits their development. We'll discuss the characteristics of twice-exceptional children, examine the strengths of twice-exceptional children have, and consider the best ways to leverage those strengths to support areas of difficulty. Part I concludes with a look specifically at how being cognitively gifted influences the development of neurodivergent children and teens.

DOI: 10.4324/9781003237532-2

1

What Is Neurodiversity?

The term neurodiversity was first coined in 1998 by a sociologist named Judy Singer. The model of neurodiversity is based on the concept that various types of "disorders" are normal variations in human development and, if provided with an environment that allows for these differences, neurodivergent people can flourish. The concept of neurodiversity rejects the pathologizing of various diagnoses.

Neurodiversity recognizes each person as an individual and knows each person has their own strengths and struggles. Being neurodivergent doesn't mean a person is broken or needs to be fixed. They need support to access the world around them. The solution to helping someone who needs a wheelchair get up steps isn't to teach them to walk; it is to build a ramp. The solution for someone who has a disability based on their neurological wiring isn't to tell them to try harder; it is to build (and help them build for themselves) accommodations that allow them to thrive.

I'm not suggesting that our twice-exceptional kids should go through life expecting the world to accommodate their every need. Expecting the world to bend over backwards to make things easy isn't realistic. But … What if we could help kids learn that their needs are valid? What if we taught them how to independently advocate for the external support they need and coached them to develop skills and strategies to manage the

DOI: 10.4324/9781003237532-3

internal skills they need? They'd be set up for success as they enter adulthood.

It is interesting to consider how neurodivergent people would fare if society weren't so rigid in its expectations. What if gifted kids weren't required to remain with their same-age peers at school and could be instructed at their cognitive level? How would simply having an appropriate educational setting shift their development? Or, what if eye contact weren't a requirement for having a successful job interview? Think of the talent companies would access! As a society, we are making progress. For example, the belief that listening to audiobooks is somehow less valuable than reading has been greatly reduced in recent years. The advocacy work of neurodiverse people is slowly changing the way we see and accept those whose neurological wiring is different.

As host of *The Neurodiversity Podcast*, I've had the chance to interview some of the most respected experts in the fields of giftedness, twice-exceptionality, and neurodiversity. For episode 74, I spoke to Steve Silberman. Steve wrote the book that introduced me to the concept of neurodiversity. His 2015 book, *Neurotribes: The Legacy of Autism and the Future of Neurodiversity*, offered an in-depth view of how people believed there was an epidemic of autism in the early 2000s, the stigma that autism has developed since it was first identified, and how damaging these beliefs were to autistic people who had immense ability to offer the world.

During our interview, Steve offered an example of how society's beliefs impact how certain concepts are pathologized and shared about his personal connection to it.

> When I was in high school, I, myself, was listed in the *Diagnostic and Statistical Manual of Mental Disorders* under homosexuality. ... I'm glad to say homosexuality is out of the DSM, and it's not because scientists discovered that, "Oh, homosexuality isn't a disorder after all." It's because gay psychiatrists and gay people flooded the offices of the APA and demanded that it be changed. ... [There's now] this wave of social awareness that's mostly driven by autistic people speaking for themselves. Now we understand

that not everything that is associated with autism is a deficit or an impairment.[1]

Within the span of his lifetime, our society has moved from pathologizing homosexuality as a mental disorder to recognizing that variations in sexual orientation are normal; now, the neurodiversity movement is moving toward destigmatizing and depathologizing various diagnoses, too.

The Language of Neurodiversity

Within the spaces of social media, there is often a lot of talk about the "right" terminology to use to describe neurodivergent individuals. Anytime we are labeling people, there are many opinions about the right language to use, and language evolves. Here are a few quick notes and observations about the language I'll be using throughout this book and why I'm using specific terminology and not others. I hope nothing changes in the time between when I write this and when the book is published!

Person-First versus Identity-First Language
Many of us are used to hearing person-first language: a student who has dyslexia or a child with autism. However, many in the neurodiversity community aren't comfortable with that language. They prefer identity-first language: a dyslexic student or an autistic child.

Person-first language indicates that somehow the label or diagnosis is separate from the person, as though we could remove that pesky autism or eliminate that attention deficit and we'd just have the neurotypical person remaining. Neurodivergence doesn't work this way. Neurological brain wiring is lifelong. It is also inherently tied to an individual's personality. A twice-exceptional person might develop coping skills and learn to navigate the world with few people noticing them, but that doesn't mean they are no longer neurodivergent.

Throughout this text, I'll use identity-first language when I'm describing neurodivergent people almost all the time. The neurodiversity community is still figuring out how to work around some labels. For example, ADHD doesn't have a simple grammatical way to change it to a personal noun. Some people have started using the term ADHDer. (Note: Interesting that nobody ever questions calling someone a gifted student, isn't it? You can see how the way we word things influences our thought processes and emotions surrounding them.)

Of course, when I'm working with a neurodivergent person, I default to the terminology they prefer. If person-first is what makes them feel comfortable, I will take the cues from them. In the same way, it is up to you and your child how you would like to talk about their specific labels. It can be an evolving conversation and is one that doesn't have a wrong answer.

Disordered or Misunderstood?

Another consideration when we are talking about the language associated with neurodiversity has to do with the term "disorder." Many of the diagnoses associated with neurodiversity come with that label slapped on the end of them: autism spectrum *disorder*, attention deficit hyperactivity *disorder*, bipolar *disorder*. If the premise of the neurodiversity movement is to normalize these conditions, the word "disorder" certainly doesn't help. As a neurodiversity-affirming therapist, I avoid using this terminology with my clients. It is unnecessary and contradicts the therapeutic goal of emphasizing that neurodiversity is normal. I will try to avoid using them in this book, too.

Fighting Functioning Labels

The final note I'll make about the language of neurodiversity has to do with functioning labels. The term Asperger's was used in prior editions of the *Diagnostic and Statistical Manual of Mental Disorders* as a neurodevelopmental diagnosis similar to autism; the main difference was that it did not include a language delay that was a requirement for a diagnosis of autism. Frequently, twice-exceptional individuals fell into this category, even using the term "Aspies" to refer to themselves. With the DSM-5's publication in 2013, Asperger's was moved under the umbrella of an autism diagnosis. The terminology high-functioning and low-functioning autism began being used, although this was never technically part of the diagnostic system. The DSM-5 indicated levels based on the amount of external support an autistic person needs for daily living (Level 1 for requiring support, Level 2 for requiring substantial support, and Level 3 for requiring very substantial support).

There are multiple problems with using functioning labels for autistic people. One of the main critiques is that it is mostly based on how much an individual's disability impacts *other* people – a person is high-functioning if their disability doesn't impact other people's ability to understand their communication or create an imposition by needing accommodations. High-functioning often is code for "mostly invisible to the outside world." However, a "high-functioning" autistic person might be struggling greatly to mask their difficulties and experiencing life that really *does* require additional support, yet, because they are supposedly "high-functioning," those accommodations may not be offered. Conversely, "low-functioning" might not be so low-functioning. For example, just because a person has difficulty with producing speech (perhaps because of muscle tone or sensory issues), doesn't mean they aren't able to advocate for themselves, navigate the world, and thrive in academic and professional environments.

One other piece of confusion that applies particularly to the twice-exceptional community is that high-functioning doesn't really mean above-average cognitive ability, although it is sometimes used that way by well-meaning people. So, when someone is described as "high-functioning," does that mean they need minimal support in their daily life, or does it mean they are very smart? Each has very different implications.

Beyond an autism diagnosis, functioning labels have also been expanded on to describe other types of diagnoses and difficulties. Perhaps you've seen articles or tweets online that describe high-functioning ADHD, depression, or anxiety. If you read these descriptions, basically what you are seeing is a person who is experiencing great internal difficulty while white-knuckling it to get through the days without allowing other people to know how much they are struggling. Many twice-exceptional people could be considered to be "high-functioning" because when you add a splash of perfectionism that often comes along with giftedness, many of us do everything possible not to allow others to see our struggles. Not only is this masking unhealthy for the individual, but it also encourages the stigma that surrounds open and honest conversations about the vulnerability of neurodiversity.

Disability Isn't a Dirty Word

As I mentioned earlier, advocates in the field of neurodiversity often push back against the term "disorder." Much of this has to do with resistance to the medical community pathologizing the needs of neurodiverse populations. Also, if a person is neurodivergent, it implies there is something wrong, disordered, or broken about their personhood, or who they are as an individual.

What may surprise some people, though, is that the neurodivergent community recognizes the term "disability" and uses it often and freely. Neurodivergent people don't deny the presence of a disability because it describes the mismatch between their skills and the situation. It allows for accommodations to provide what is needed to successfully navigate the environment. Calling it something like being "differently-abled" minimizes and infantilizes neurodivergent folks' needs. Pretending a disability only provides strengths ("ADHD is my superpower") reinforces the idea that neurodivergent people should be able to use willpower alone to overcome their disability.

Recognizing a disability requires us to become comfortable with vulnerability. Self-advocacy begins with recognizing disability without shame. When we give our children permission to recognize their difficulties, we liberate them to ask for accommodations. We empower them to look beyond the status quo and find the solutions that work for them, instead of trying to use the solutions that work for other people. And we provide a framework for self-understanding and self-acceptance that is the key for neurodivergent people of all ages.

Self-Diagnosis through Your Child's Diagnosis

Many of us grew up at a time when many types of neurodivergence weren't understood or recognized, especially in twice-exceptional people. ADHD was thought to be predominantly present in boys until recently. Autism diagnoses were reserved for individuals with significant, noticeable outward signs until an awareness of the subtleties of those traits grew. There are still people (educators!) who believe one can't both be gifted and have a learning disability. And giftedness frequently still goes unnoticed if other factors cover it up.

Often, after a child has been identified as twice-exceptional, their parent has a light bulb moment where everything clicks. They realize why they struggled so much in school or why they still feel overwhelmed by certain situations. The emotions surrounding this realization range from relief at finally having an explanation for something that had been present for so long to grief due to the time lost and lifetime of difficulty without an explanation.

If you find yourself looking back on your own experiences and identifying that the struggles your child is facing are reflective of your own, don't shy away. The journey of parenthood involves degrees of self-awareness which may have remained hidden forever without our children acting as a mirror to our own experiences. You'll be able to use this understanding to support your child and empathize with them.

This new self-awareness can feel confusing and leave a person uncertain about what to do with the information. Some parents seek a formal diagnosis for their own twice-exceptionality; others are satisfied by simply having a greater understanding for themselves. While a formal diagnosis of twice-exceptionality is validating, it can be difficult to find. The process can be cost prohibitive and often isn't covered by insurance; additionally, professionals who understand neurodiversity, giftedness, and twice-exceptionality are few and far between.

Occasionally, late-diagnosed adults feel angry, frustrated, or disappointed that their needs weren't recognized when they were young. Going through life as a neurodivergent person and not getting the support or education needed has long-lasting effects. The injustice of growing up in a world where you believed you were bad, lazy, or unmotivated, when what you really needed was some basic support and accommodations, stings. These complicated emotions are normal.

If you've realized your own neurodivergence along the way, welcome to the club. I hope this new knowledge of your neurodivergence, whether it is giftedness, autism, ADHD, or any other combination of flavors, empowers you to better understand yourself and connect to your child.

Chapter Reflection

Ask yourself these questions to gain a better self-awareness and find areas where you'd like to shift your thinking or actions:

- ◆ How has the world changed in its understanding of neurodiversity throughout your lifetime? What changes in your own beliefs have you made?
- ◆ What language do you use to describe your child's struggles and strengths? What emotions does the terminology you use evoke?
- ◆ What have you learned about yourself through parenting your twice-exceptional child? How has parenting changed you?

Note

1. Silberman, S. (2021, January 7). Autism's history and neurodiversity's future [Audio blog interview]. Retrieved from https://neurodiversitypodcast.com/home/2021/1/7/episode-74-autisms-history-and-neurodiversitys-future

2

Gifted and . . .

Dr. Susan Baum is one of the pioneers in bringing an understanding of twice-exceptional learners to the fields of psychology and gifted education. Dr. Baum was a guest on *The Neurodiversity Podcast* on episode 65 and described twice-exceptional learners as complex layers of abilities and difficulties.

> [Twice-exceptional children are cognitively advanced], but they also have at the same time some sort of learning or behavioral or attentional challenge. And we, when we put those two seemingly paradoxical pieces together we have a very unique individual. So unique that we tend to call these kids green. Because they have this yellow about them, all those advanced abilities, and yet they have this blue side that's much more problematic. And when you put those pieces together, it's hard to see yellow and blue, you keep seeing green, which makes them an extremely unique population of kids.[1]

When I started my master's program in education with certification in gifted education, it was the early 2000s. I took classes on creating curriculum for gifted learners, understanding the social and emotional development of gifted students, and more. The term "twice-exceptional" was never mentioned. We

DOI: 10.4324/9781003237532-4

talked about our own experiences with gifted students who struggled with perfectionism or lack of motivation, but the idea that a student could be both gifted and dyslexic wasn't discussed, not to mention the other types of twice-exceptional learners that exist.

From my own personal experience as a gifted/ADHD student, I knew we were out there, and I wanted to reach the kids like myself who had a really tough time getting through the educational system. Little did I know at the time how many of us there were!

In the last twenty years, educators who work in gifted education have made a lot of progress in understanding and advocating for gifted learners. However, teachers who aren't in gifted education classrooms, school administrators, and school counselors and mental health professionals are often unaware of the presence of these complex learners; most of the general public is also oblivious to the existence of twice-exceptional folks. (The number of people who deny the existence of gifted kids/adults alone is staggering; convincing these same people that giftedness can coexist with disability is a daunting task.)

As awareness for twice-exceptional people grows, so do the resources available. Schools are beginning to identify and provide services for 2e kids. Mental health professionals are starting to see that the overall wellness and mental health of twice-exceptional people are influenced by the coexistence of their diverse skill levels. Parents are learning that being labeled as gifted doesn't always mean everything comes easy.

Completing educational assessments at my office gives me a glimpse into a child's experience in the world. Some students have skills consistent across domains, with scores in each composite area falling within a few points of each other. Assuming those scores are average or above, these students feel comfortable meeting the academic challenges presented to them in the classroom. The twice-exceptional student has a spiky profile, full of peaks and valleys of strengths and weaknesses. One area that appears to be a strength is hindered by another area of weakness, and the discomfort of trying to compensate for areas of impeded ability is often overwhelming.

The Typical Atypical 2e Child

It is practically impossible to lump together all twice-exceptional learners and give generalizations about an entire group. The intersectionality of cognitive ability, neurodivergence, personality, and environmental influences creates a combination of traits that makes each twice-exceptional person completely unique. However, a general framework for understanding the nuances of twice-exceptionality is useful to put your child's characteristics into context and start to develop an idea of how to support them. Chapter 3 will delve into the various diagnoses that can be combined with giftedness to produce a twice-exceptional profile.

Asynchronous Development

In the field of gifted education, we talk a lot about asynchronous development. Asynchronous development is when a child has varying levels of ability in different areas of their lives. For example, an 8-year-old gifted child may have the language and critical thinking skills of a 15-year-old child, but their fine motor skills and executive functioning skills are commensurate for their chronological age. Twice-exceptional kids often have even more variation because of their disability. Their social skills or emotional regulation skills may be lower than their actual age and on par with a typically developing 6-year-old.

This dichotomy is confusing for parents and teachers. Many gifted children tend to get held to a higher standard for behavior than their same-age peers because they often "appear" so much older and more mature based on their language skill, even though their social and emotional development isn't as advanced. They talk like little mini-lawyers, but then have an emotional breakdown when their point isn't understood or accepted. Understanding the asynchrony of gifted and twice-exceptional learners is important to support their development.

A Quick Look at Intelligence and IQ Scores

If your child has been identified as gifted, it is likely that they've had some kind of intelligence test. The concept of g in psychology represents the idea that there is a general intelligence among humans that exists among humans. "IQ" is the tool we've created to attempt to measure intelligence. While there are definitely flaws in IQ tests, they are one of the most consistently tested and validated constructs in psychology. Russell Warne talked about the various types of IQ measures that are used in the world and how almost all of them are able to consistently measure the concept of *g* on episode 69 of the podcast.

> We eventually found 97 archival data sets from 31 of these nations. They're in South America, Central America, sub-Saharan Africa, the Arab world, South Asia, Oceania, basically anywhere that's not majority European. ... We ran the factor analysis, and in over 95% of the data sets, we found *g*. Even though there are important differences in what cultures see as intelligent behavior, and even though there are important differences in what the word intelligence might mean, that statistical abstraction, the *g*, that's present, there seems to be one broad ability that people worldwide use to solve cognitive problems.[2]

What does intelligence really tell us? In general, a person who scores highly on an intelligence test is able to make abstract connections between concepts, use logic to discover patterns and similarities in images, and show a depth of knowledge that is beyond what most people of a similar age show. Intelligent people learn new concepts rapidly and find novel solutions to problems. Intelligence doesn't always tell us how well a child will do in school.

We are facing a crisis of anti-intellectualism in the United States, and the students who are being hurt the most are bright kids who don't fit the stereotype of high achievers in our schools. As more districts and states pull back from providing gifted services in the name of equity, the kids who are going to be hurt the most are the ones who *need* those services the most. Students from culturally and linguistically diverse backgrounds, economically disadvantaged students, and neurodivergent kids are the kids who will fall through the cracks. The bright students who excel in the academic setting and those who have parents who can pay for private schools or extra enrichment outside of school will be fine (although they deserve to be challenged, too). I'm always floored when educational advocates somehow believe that eliminating opportunities for bright learners (like getting rid of gifted programs) is going to make the situation better. If there is inequity in a program, let's fix the inequity by improving identification methods and giving more students the opportunity to participate. The more options and opportunities the better!

I'll be the first to say that just because a child has an IQ score that qualifies them for a certain program or service doesn't necessarily mean it is a good fit for them. There is so much variance between gifted programs and the types of services that are offered. Some programs offer the flexibility to both accommodate a child's areas of difficulty while using their strengths to push them forward. Some states even provide an individualized learning plan (ILP) for gifted students, allowing a program to be created with goals specific to their abilities and needs. (If you live in one of those states, consider yourself one of the lucky ones!)

Most gifted programs offer services to students who have an IQ in the top 2–5% of all students. Students who score at or above the 95th percentile have an IQ of ≥124; students who score at or above the 98th percentile have an IQ of ≥130. But the varying strengths a child might have to reach this score can vary greatly. The Wechsler Intelligence Scale for Children (WISC-V) is the most commonly used assessment for measuring IQ in children. There are five composite scores that are combined to create the Full Scale IQ. Each composite measures a different type of cognitive skill and tells us something different about a child's overall learning profile.

Understanding what a cognitive assessment means is useful because you and your child's teachers can use this information to better understand why some things may appear easier than others for your child. It can help to drive the ways you support your child at home and at school. However, one cognitive assessment doesn't define your child. There are twice-exceptional children

Composite score	What it measures	What it means	Possible impact on 2e learners
Verbal Comprehension	Measures a child's knowledge of language, vocabulary, and their ability to use language to explain abstract concepts	Children with strong Verbal Comprehension scores do well with language-based learning, such as reading, writing, or speaking.	2e learners with weaker Verbal Comprehension skills may struggle in advanced learning programs that are focused on language-based skills. Some 2e learners may have strong Verbal Comprehension skills while also having a learning disability (like dyslexia) that inhibits their ability to perform on some academic tasks.
Visual-Spatial	Measures a child's ability to use reasoning skills to solve problems that require an ability to see and manipulate items in space	Kids with strong Visual-Spatial skills often enjoy LEGOs and puzzles. At school, they may perform well with visual arts or geometry.	Twice-exceptional learners with a profile showing strength in the Visual-Spatial domain alongside relative weaknesses in the other areas may perceive tasks related to verbal skills as more difficult.
Fluid Reasoning	Measures a child's ability to analyze and comprehend abstract patterns and implement inductive/deductive reasoning to extrapolate information to the next logical step in a pattern or analogy	Students with strong Fluid Reasoning skills make novel connections between concepts that seem unrelated or create new solutions to problems they've not been exposed to before.	Fluid Reasoning requires a level of flexibility and openness to new solutions to problems. Students who prefer tasks with a clear right or wrong answer (without the need to make inferences) may struggle when assessed for Fluid Reasoning skills.

Working Memory	Measures a child's ability to hold and manipulate information in their short-term memory	Working Memory is related to reasoning skills due to the ability to maintain access to or disengage with information that is relevant to the problem-solving process. For example, students participating in an oral debate need to access their working memory to recall all of the topics being discussed.	Some neurodivergent people have Working Memory difficulties. This can impact executive functioning skills or following multi-step instructions. Academically, Working Memory skills are needed in reading, where someone must maintain information in their short-term memory to make inferences, and writing, to put one's thoughts into sequence and get them onto paper.
Processing Speed	Measures a child's ability to receive, interpret, and react to information	Students with strong Processing Speed are able to receive visual or auditory information and contextualize it quickly. They do not require extra "think time" before responding to a question or request and are able to complete work quickly (and accurately).	Processing Speed is another area where neurodivergent children frequently need support. This might mean extra time on assignments or tests or a slower conversation pace to allow time to process the information shared and construct a response. Additionally, students who struggle significantly with anxiety/perfectionism may have slower Processing Speed as they are very cautious when replying and spend additional time ensuring accurate responses.

TABLE 2.1 Understanding IQ score composites in 2e learners

(Continued)

Composite score	What it measures	What it means	Possible impact on 2e learners
Full Scale IQ	A composite score including components of all the above areas gives an overall view of a child's general cognitive ability.	Students with strong FSIQ scores typically have above average scores in each of the composite areas that combine to create this score.	The FSIQ (or GAI) is generally used as a benchmark for a child's ability, assuming a child's achievement in academic areas should approach their overall ability (FSIQ). Twice-exceptional kids with a big gap between their FSIQ and other achievement scores may be exhibiting signs of a learning disability.
General Ability Index	A composite score including only scores from Verbal Comprehension, Visual-Spatial, and Fluid Reasoning scales.	It is common for many high-ability students to have Working Memory and Processing Speed scores that develop more slowly based on their chronological age, although these scores may not indicate their ability to complete complex cognitive tasks, like those provided in gifted education programs.	The GAI tends to be a better measure of overall cognitive ability for many neurodivergent students because it eliminates the Working Memory and Processing Speed scores, which are frequently lower than the other areas of ability measured by a cognitive assessment.

TABLE 2.1 (Cont.)

out there whose scores on a cognitive assessment are suppressed and don't capture the impact of, for example, an area of passion that might push a child to perform beyond what an assessment says they should be able to do. Cognitive assessments are like a snapshot of how a child is doing the day they are assessed, impacted by their mood, motivation, confidence, and willingness to take risks.

Some people refer to the learning profile of a twice-exceptional learner as a "spiky" profile, meaning there are lots of peaks and valleys in their abilities. Schools are set up to teach to the middle of the bell curve – the majority of the people who have similar needs that develop at a similar rate. 68% of people have IQs between 85 and 115; 95% of people have IQs between 70 and 130. Achievement scores (in academic areas, like reading and math) typically align with one's overall ability, however, a twice-exceptional student may have scores all over the place. It is understandable that it makes it difficult for our schools to match instruction to students whose needs vary so greatly and are often at odds with each other.

Knowing that your child has a unique learning profile will allow you to understand and support them. It can help you have compassion for their difficulties, find creative ways to foster their strengths, and support the things that don't come so easily. When we're working with twice-exceptional kids, the best place to start is by developing their strengths.

Start with the Strengths

Throughout this book, there will be ideas and strategies that you can use to support your twice-exceptional child. All of them begin with one single premise: Presume competence. We are going to operate from the assumption that our children want to do well, they are motivated to succeed, and they just need some support to get there. Presuming competence means kids do well when they have the skills necessary for a task and we may need to work with them to figure out what accommodations they need. Presuming competence takes a conversation from, "Why can't you/won't you just do this task?" to, "I know you can do this. What do you need to be able to accomplish it?"

Presuming competence also requires us to begin with the strengths that our children have and use them as a launching pad for moving them toward independence. These strengths might be interest-based. How can you take a child's fascination in computer coding or ecology and integrate those interests into the skill-building of other tasks? Maybe they can create a computer code in Scratch to create a checklist they can use to monitor executive functioning skills, or they can find ways to build math skills through developing a plan to improve the environment around their school. You could also consider strategies and skills they have already established as strengths and maximize those to improve other skills. Does your child do well with routines and consistency? You could use this preference to create routines surrounding areas of difficulty, delineating and breaking down the various tasks in discrete steps in a consistent routine. Is your child a creative and divergent thinker? Let them come up with novel and new ways to attempt certain tasks through their own creative process and encourage them to revisit the plan with renewed creative problem solving if its effectiveness dulls over time.

Twice-exceptional children have many strengths, and assessing those strengths will help you find a starting point to support them. The common thread that all twice-exceptional children have as a strength is their cognitive ability. Their cognitive ability gives us several areas we can use as assets as we work with them.

- ◆ Quick learning pace: Gifted learners are generally able to integrate new information and complex topics quickly.
- ◆ Strong verbal abilities: Many gifted learners have strong verbal skills, so they can comprehend advanced concepts easily (although some twice-exceptional learners may have difficulty expressing their own thoughts in words, either verbally or in writing).

◆ Strong logic and reasoning skills: Providing facts and information about a topic (or better yet, letting them research it themselves) gives opportunities to implement their ability to analyze evidence to support their conclusions.

◆ Divergent thinking skills: Looking at problems in multiple ways to try to experiment to find new strategies that might work is another way to harness a trait of giftedness.

◆ Big picture thinkers: Twice-exceptional learners have the ability to understand the "big picture," and contextualizing information to know why certain skills are important is important to motivation for them.

Table 2.2 gives some ideas of questions to ask about your child's personality and learning profile to help you examine what starting points might be useful as you work to maximize your child's strengths.

Ask yourself or your child ...	Use this information to ...
What is your child interested in learning? How does your child spend their free time?	Tie in their areas of interest to the skill you are trying to build.
What academic areas in school come easily?	Integrate skills from academic areas that don't come as easily to the areas that are stronger.
Does your child thrive on novelty and change?	Change things up to keep your child's interest and engagement; don't continue trying to use a strategy that is no longer working.
Does your child prefer the comfort of consistency?	Provide advance notice of changes (in writing, if it is helpful) and keep things as routine as possible to prevent unexpected changes.
How does your child best communicate?	Give your child permission to choose how they like to have difficult conversations. Perhaps they prefer to write notes in a shared journal, text, or talk one-on-one before bed.

TABLE 2.2 Maximizing your child's strengths

Social and Emotional Considerations for Gifted Children

When "Because I Said So" Doesn't Work

One of the most popular presentations I give for parents of gifted kids is all about how to understand the communication style and cognitive needs of their children. Gifted kids will never be the kids who are satisfied with the response "because I said so." We've all been there and uttered the phrase with the intent to shut down a conversation. Perhaps your child complied, or perhaps they argued. Their cognitive profile is analyzing every angle of a conversation and working to integrate the information into their understanding of the world, and if something doesn't make sense to them, telling them "because I said so" isn't going to get you too far. Taking the time to explain our thinking helps them learn that even if they don't agree with your resolution, they can contextualize it within the bigger picture of what they understand about the world, you, and your relationship with them.

Gifted education has advocated for support for gifted learners on the basis of their social and emotional needs for a long time under the assumption that the simple fact that being gifted comes along with inherent needs that aren't met in a typical education classroom. However, as more research is completed, it appears that giftedness is a protective factor for most people, as opposed to a risk factor.[3] This is good news for gifted education advocates everywhere because it actually gives us a stronger advocacy point for support services, stating that the mismatch between services and gifted students is the cause of many difficulties for gifted learners; if a bright child is placed in a supportive, flexible, and challenging classroom environment, we can reduce the negative outcomes classically ascribed to gifted individuals, like perfectionism, anxiety, or underachievement.

Since we have yet to achieve this level of accommodation for our bright learners, there are some social and emotional considerations that are unique to the gifted population and are worth noting.

◆ Perfectionism: While it is important to note that unhealthy perfectionism is not exclusive to gifted populations, research does show increased perfectionistic strivings.[4]

When gifted kids learn rapidly, they expect things to continue to come easily to them. When eventually they face a challenge, they may feel overwhelmed because this is a risk to their self-image. They internalize the message that learning things is easy and integrate it into their identity without experiencing the need for resilience when facing difficult tasks. Opportunities to take risks and permission to fail can help prevent developing overwhelming perfectionism. Additionally, learning how to effectively ask for help is a crucial skill for kids with perfectionistic tendencies (see Chapter 7).

◆ Heightened emotional sensitivity: Defined by Sal Mendaglio as heightened multifaceted sensitivity, gifted individuals face "enhanced awareness of behavior, emotions, and cognitions pertaining to self and others."[5] Without the life experience behind them to understand how to get through difficult situations and the cognitive ability to understand the big picture and overall long-term impact events might have, gifted kids can feel helpless and overwhelmed by their emotions. A sense of autonomy and volition in their lives can help to reduce negative emotional intensity because kids feel empowered to act when they see things that are unjust, whether in their own lives or greater society.

◆ Underachievement: Gifted kids who underachieve are often products of environments that have failed to provide appropriate levels of challenge or have misjudged the appropriate level of challenge and placed a student in an environment that is too much of a stretch for their ability. Twice-exceptional children often are labeled underachievers because of an undiagnosed disability.

Because of their dual labels, twice-exceptional children will face many of these issues (and others) through the lens of both the giftedness and disability. Additionally, the broad umbrella of twice-exceptionality adds in its own specific social and emotional needs, based on the specific diagnosis. These are addressed throughout the book in relation to specific diagnoses (Chapter 3) and in the various chapters on helping 2e kids build the skills they need for success.

Chapter Reflection

- ◆ Where do you see your child's asynchrony?
- ◆ When do you see your child utilizing their strengths to compensate for areas of difficulty?
- ◆ How can you help them leverage their strengths in new ways in different environments (home, school, social relationships)?

Notes

1. Baum, S. (2020, August 19). A talk with a 2e pioneer [Audio blog interview]. Retrieved from https://neurodiversitypodcast.com/home/2020/8/19/episode-65-a-talk-with-a-2e-pioneer

2. Warne, R. (2020, October 14). Sifting through IQ: What we know about intelligence [Audio blog interview]. Retrieved from https://neurodiversitypodcast.com/home/2020/10/14/episode-69-sifting-through-iq-what-we-know-about-intelligence

3. Suldo, S. M., Hearon, B. V., & Shaunessy-Dedrick, E. (2018). Examining gifted students' mental health through the lens of positive psychology. In APA handbook of giftedness and talent (pp. 433–449). Washington, DC: American Psychological Association.

4. Stricker, J., Buecker, S., Schneider, M., & Preckel, F. (2019). Intellectual giftedness and multidimensional perfectionism: A meta-analytic review. Educational Psychology Review, 32(2), 391–414. doi:10.1007/s10648–019–09504–1

5. Mendaglio, S. (2010). Affective-cognitive therapy for counseling gifted individuals. In Models of counseling gifted children, adolescents, and young adults (pp. 35–68). Waco, TX: Prufrock Press.

3

Identifying and Understanding Twice-Exceptionality

This chapter gives brief descriptions of the possible variations of twice-exceptionality our neurodivergent kids might face. I want to be sure to clarify that this is in no way a comprehensive list. I'll share some ways that giftedness may mask another type of neurodivergence or vice versa and other considerations you may want to include as you are seeking support for your child. It is important to point out that the term "twice-exceptional" is a bit of a misnomer because children aren't limited to only two types of exceptionalities. "Multi-exceptional" is a better term, although infrequently used, because there are many neurodivergent 2e learners who are gifted/ADHD/autistic or gifted/autistic/dysgraphic, to name a few examples. Comorbidities, as coexisting diagnoses are called in the medical field, are common.

There is a saying in the autistic community: "If you've met one autistic person, you've met one autistic person." The same goes for 2e learners. There are some generalizations that can help us figure out how to support them, but we want to be careful about generalizing too much.

There has been a major push to be wary of misdiagnosis in the gifted community. While it is important not to pathologize

DOI: 10.4324/9781003237532-5

traits of giftedness, some of the hesitance people experience about giving a diagnosis to a gifted child is based in fear and stigmatization of certain types of neurodiversity. I've worked with families who are very resistant to any type of label (other than giftedness). Instead of the misdiagnosis they want to avoid, they end up with a missed diagnosis, which is often equally (or more) damaging to the child's development.

One of the major influences in the field of giftedness that drives missed diagnosis is the misinterpretation of overexcitabilities. Overexcitabilities (also known as "super-sensitivities") are often cited and discussed in the bubble of gifted education, however, within the wider field of psychology are essentially unknown. The research supporting overexcitabilities is scarce, and the results available are mixed. Understandably, many families prefer to think that a child who is unable to sit still and maintain attention is dealing with a trait of giftedness – psychomotor overexcitability – rather than an attention deficit. It is also easier to believe that because a child is gifted, they experience intense sensory sensitivities (tags in clothes, seams in socks) due to their sensual overexcitability instead of considering the possibility that their child is gifted/autistic and experiences hyper-reactivity to sensory input. There is some evidence of increased sensitivity to sensory stimuli in individuals with advanced cognitive abilities,[1] however, if it is causing daily distress, we shouldn't write it off.

The trouble with a missed diagnosis is that we lose the opportunity to be proactive in supporting our children. Children with advanced cognitive abilities are generally diagnosed much later than their same-age peers because their abilities mask their difficulties. For example, a gifted/dyslexic child may struggle greatly with reading fluency and phonological awareness, however, because they have strong background knowledge and inferencing skills, they may appear "on grade level" for overall reading skills. When we finally recognize the presence of a learning disability, we have lost years of time to utilize the exceptional neuroplasticity of young children to build strong foundational skills necessary for advanced reading. What is the long-term effect of an internalized belief that you don't like to read? What opportunities for future classes or career paths may be lost by not recognizing the struggle and calling it what it is as soon as possible?

A misdiagnosis is also problematic, for obvious reasons. First, a misdiagnosis can eclipse a child's ability and be a barrier to their giftedness ever being noticed. Another possibility is that a misdiagnosis is trying to solve the wrong problems. What happens when a gifted/autistic child is wrongly identified as an ADHDer? Or a gifted/ADHDer is diagnosed as a child with a mood disorder? I've seen situations like these occur more than once and giftedness complicates the diagnostic process.

The Social Model of Disability

The concept of neurodiversity is based on the social model of disability. Whereas the medical model of disability looks for differences in levels of functioning and ability and attempts to bring them into alignment with what is considered "normal," the social model of disability recognizes the limitations caused by a disability when society is unsupportive of an individual's impairments. For example, a person who is deaf is only dis-abled when accommodations for closed captioning or a sign language interpreter aren't made. If society were to make these accommodations accessible, their impairment would be minimized, and they would be able to access the world as easily as non-disabled people.

Related to neurodiversity, the social model of disability also values the differences that make a person neurodivergent and suggests that neurodiversity is a normal part of human variation and is a necessary and vital component of human survival. John Elder Robison is an autistic adult, author, and neurodiversity advocate. Speaking of neurodiversity, he said, "many individuals who embrace the concept of neurodiversity believe that people with differences do not need to be cured; they need help and accommodation instead. They look at the pool of diverse humanity and see – in the middle – the range of different thinking that's made humanity's progress in science and the creative arts possible. … When 99 neurologically identical people fail to solve a problem, it's often the 1% fellow who's different who holds the key."[2]

Who is a 3e Learner?

Twice-exceptional learners from culturally or linguistically diverse backgrounds face additional challenges in being identified as 2e and receiving services. The field of gifted education is currently grappling with the reality of its past failures to identify students from minoritized populations. The term "3e" is used to identify twice-exceptional students who also have another type of diversity that influences their access to services. Dr. Joy Lawson Davis was one of the first people to start writing about gifted students of color who also have another diagnosis. On episode 63 of *The Neurodiversity Podcast*, she shared about the impact of not identifying twice-exceptional students of color. "We know we're not doing the best thing we can do for students of color, culturally diverse, black students, brown students, because they are still being overlooked. And, unfortunately when we overlook them, we under-identify them, then that's a great loss of talent, not only to the individual, but to the community, to the world at large."[3] Practices to screen all students for giftedness and remove assessment practices that can be impacted by implicit bias (like teacher referrals) are one step schools are taking to prevent this talent from being overlooked.

Understanding Giftedness

The factor common to each of the types of twice-exceptionality that we'll discuss through this book is that each has cognitive ability that is far above average compared to their same-age peers. What is "gifted" can often be a moving target. Since giftedness isn't a formal psychological diagnosis or label, it often falls to the schools to identify gifted/talented learners, but there isn't even an agreed-upon benchmark for what is "gifted" in schools.[4] Many schools use some type of a cognitive assessment (aka IQ test) and have settled on providing gifted services for the top 2–10% of learners, although many schools are moving to alternate identification measures to improve and expand gifted services.

Giftedness is a broad description for a wide range of skills which vary greatly between individuals. In the educational world, giftedness is often tied to academic achievement; as the parent of a twice-exceptional child, you probably recognize that academic achievement and giftedness aren't always a package deal. Some of the skills exhibited by gifted people include advanced abstract reasoning skills, strong logical thinking ability, or sophisticated verbal comprehension.

Attention Deficit/Hyperactivity (Disorder)

If you have an ADHD child, they fall into one of three categories of ADHD: predominantly inattentive type (the daydreamer), predominantly hyperactive type (the Energizer bunny), or combined type (a little bit of both). Attention deficit/hyperactivity is a misnomer because it implies that an ADHDer has a deficit of attention. Rather than having *not enough* attention to stay focused, ADHDers have a combination of *too much* attention (noticing everything in their environment) coupled with an *inability to regulate* their attention or focus (tuning out the extraneous stuff and consciously choosing where to direct their attention).

It is confusing when parents see a child who can focus for hours on LEGO or video games, but can't manage to follow a simple routine to get ready in time for the bus in the morning. When considering if someone is struggling with an attention deficit, consider whether they can self-regulate their focus on a nonpreferred activity. Being able to focus on something you love is easy; the ability to regulate your focus on a task that isn't self-selected is a better measure of attention concerns. Some people describe ADHDers having difficulty with hyper-focusing on a task – that is, being so focused on a task they are unaware of what is happening around them. This is another example of an inability to regulate focus or intentionally direct attention where it is needed.

Gifted/ADHD 2e kids are the students who never manage to turn in their homework, yet ace the tests. Their giftedness might mask their attention difficulties because they can essentially hear only about twenty percent of the classroom instruction and still get by. As rigor increases and the requirements for success in classes becomes more reliant on executive functioning skills, these gifted/ADHD kids are no longer able to manage the expectations without support and accommodations.

Creativity and divergent thinking are two areas where gifted/ADHD folks have an advantage over others. It is well documented that ADHDers show increased creativity compared to non-ADHD peers.[5] 2e gifted/ADHD learners also tend to be intuitive, big picture thinkers. They might get bogged down in the details, but their motivation to solve problems in new and unique ways is a drive we can harness.

Part of the brain chemistry that causes difficulty for these neurodivergent people is related to dopamine. Dopamine is called the reward chemical of the brain, initiating feelings of wellbeing and accomplishment. ADHDers tend to have a lower-than-normal number of dopamine transporters. Without these dopamine transporters, ADHDers don't get the same sense of satisfaction experience as non-ADHDers from completing a mundane task, like emptying the dishwasher or organizing their backpack. Medication for ADHD focuses on increasing the levels of dopamine by promoting increased dopamine release from the synapses of the brain. Some medications also work by blocking the dopamine from being reabsorbed into the brain too soon. Norepinephrine is another brain chemical targeted by stimulant medications for ADHD.

A lot of the neurological action described above is taking place in the pre-frontal cortex of the brain, which is responsible for executive functioning skills (like time management, task initiation, prioritizing, response inhibition, and organization). Dopamine and norepinephrine are like the grease that helps the gears run smoothly; ADHDers who struggle with these tasks aren't being difficult because they are lazy or apathetic; their brains just aren't wired that way.

Knowing this about ADHD brains, you can see why ADHDers tend to thrive in new, novel environments and can be thrill-seekers. The new experiences are exciting, triggering those feel-good chemicals that day-to-day, repetitive tasks lack. The inability to sustain attention to mundane or tedious tasks causes difficulties in academic, professional, and social environments if accommodations aren't available and self-advocacy skills are lacking.

While not a component of the diagnostic criteria for ADHD, emotional regulation difficulties are common in ADHDers. One common manifestation of emotional dysregulation in ADHDers is sensitivity to perceived rejection. This is sometimes called rejection sensitivity dysphoria. Research shows that kids who exhibit notable ADHD symptoms have heightened negative reactions to peer rejection and reduced positive reactions when peers accept them.[6] In addition to difficulties within friendships, this exaggerated response to discouraging reactions from those around them can cause ADHDers to react with intense emotions to even mild criticism from parents, teachers, or other adults. Chapter 5 looks at how parents can help to build connection through communication, which is useful for kids who struggle with rejection sensitivity; Chapter 8 gives ideas specifically about building emotional regulation skills.

Autism Spectrum

When I started my clinical practice, my intent was to specialize in supporting the mental health of gifted individuals. I had no idea that autism would become both an area of specialization and passion. However, a large percentage of my caseload gradually ended up being made up of autistic clients, and my immersion into the world of neurodiversity began.

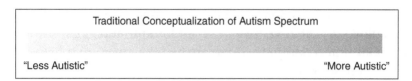

FIGURE 3.1 The traditional conceptualization of the autism spectrum gives the perception that there is a linear path from "less autistic" to "more autistic."

Prior to the fifth edition of *Diagnostic and Statistical Manual of Mental Disorders* (DSM-5) being published in 2013, these clients generally had a diagnosis of Asperger's disorder; the new DSM-5 included Asperger's beneath the diagnosis of autism spectrum. While autism is described as a spectrum, it is helpful to realize that conceptualizing it as a linear spectrum from more severe to less severe autism can be misleading. A more useful visualization of how the autism spectrum manifests is a circle, with the various areas of specific needs segmented like pieces of a pie (see Figure 3.2). The various areas that impact individuals are diverse, and the levels of support they need also vary. The terms "high-functioning" and "low-functioning" have fallen out of favor in the neurodiversity community because they are extremely limited in the information they provide. An autistic person may be nonspeaking yet need limited support; conversely, another autistic person may appear to be very "high-functioning" but need significant support in their daily lives. (Note: functioning labels are also confusing when we are discussing twice-exceptional learners because "high-functioning" is often conflated with high intelligence/cognitive ability, although it does not have that meaning in the autistic community.)

Autism impacts an individual in two main areas. The first area is related specifically to communication. Autistic individuals may not naturally engage in common neurotypical styles of reciprocal conversation, and talking about and expressing their emotions may be difficult, either because doing so causes feelings of overwhelm or because they find it difficult to specifically identify their emotions. Interpreting the underlying intent of someone's communication may be unclear for autistic people because recognizing and using nonverbal communication isn't

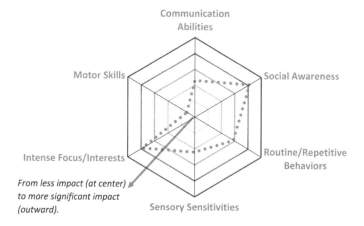

FIGURE 3.2 Understanding the autism spectrum as a multi-dimensional profile instead of a linear scale helps to conceptualize the varying strengths and struggles each autistic person may experience.

as automatic. Perspective taking by predicting other people's thoughts and emotions can also cause difficulty in communicating; this specific difficulty is related to a concept known as "theory of mind." Some people interpret this difficulty as a lack of empathy; however, many autistic individuals are extremely empathetic. (For a discussion on the differences between cognitive and affective empathy, see Chapter 10.)

The second area most impacted for autistic people is related to "repetitive and restrictive patterns of behavior." For example, repetitive motor movements, such as waving one's hands, pacing, or rocking can be calming for autistic people. These behaviors are also known as "stims" or "stimming," and autistic people describe these motor movements as helpful for emotional regulation. Consistency with routines and repetitive behaviors are often comforting to autistic people, and unexpected changes and transitions without advance notice, planning, or support can cause distress. Interests that are extremely intense are satisfying to autistic people, and they may prefer to focus on them exclusively. However, in certain social situations or settings where focus on other topics is necessary (like school) this can be problematic. Sensory differences are another area where autistic brains differ from neurotypical brains. Sensory-avoidance can be related to feeling overwhelmed by bright lights, noises, smells, or textures; sensory-seeking might be exhibited by fascination with touching certain surfaces or choosing activities like swinging at recess. Sensory differences can also take the form of differences in how an autistic person experiences pain and expresses sensory experiences.

More than Just the Five Senses

Sensory sensitivities for autistic people can manifest in areas beyond just the five senses. Table 3.1 is a (non-exhaustive) list of possible ways a neurodivergent person may experience sensory input differently. (Note: other neurodivergent people, like ADHDers, often have sensory experiences that are different than neurotypicals' experiences although it is not a component of the diagnostic criteria in the DSM-5.)

Tactile (touch)	◆ Sensitivity to certain types of fabrics, tags in clothing, seams in socks (avoidant) ◆ Touches items or others frequently (seeking)
Auditory (hearing)	◆ Avoidance of loud or noisy environments (avoidant) ◆ Hyperawareness of background noises in environment, like the buzz from fluorescent lights or people eating (avoidant)
Visual (sight)	◆ Low tolerance for bright lights (avoidant) ◆ Likes bright, reflective, or spinning objects (seeking)
Gustatory (taste)	◆ Avoidance of certain tastes and flavors; preferring bland foods (avoidant) ◆ Prefers strong flavors, tastes nonfood items (seeking)
Olfactory (smell)	◆ Low tolerance for strong smells, like perfumes or candles (avoidant) ◆ Comforted by scent on familiar objects, like clothing or favorite stuffed animals (seeking)
Proprioceptive (body awareness)	◆ Prefers to run, jump, stomp (seeking) or tiptoe (avoidant), rather than walking ◆ Enjoys deep pressure, such as tight hugs or weighted blankets (seeking)

TABLE 3.1 Examples of sensory sensitivities

Vestibular (movement)	◆ Rocks or swings in chair (seeking) ◆ Refuses to participate in PE or playground games (avoidant)
Interoceptive (internal systems)	◆ Difficulty recognizing symptoms from one's body; for example, inability to differentiate between feeling sick, hungry, or needing to use the bathroom ◆ Low awareness of body cues of emotions; for example, not noticing heart rate increasing when feeling scared (this impacts one's ability to proactively regulate emotions)

TABLE 3.1 (Cont.)

Many gifted/autistic individuals tend to mask their neurodivergence in order to blend into the world around them. A bright child who is frequently told to make eye contact or stop waving their hands is likely to learn ways to suppress the tendency to look away from someone's eyes or resist the desire to stim, even if it increases their anxiety or discomfort. Some therapies, such as applied behavioral analysis (ABA), use discrete trial training and tangible reinforcements (aka rewards and punishments) to decrease certain behaviors. For autistic children, this type of therapy removes their autonomy and agency, attempting to use behavioral techniques rewire their neurology. Autistic adults who've experienced ABA therapy talk about the traumatization they've experienced through this type of therapy and compare it to conversion therapy in the LGBTQ+ community. Instead of this type of behavior therapy, autistic kids are better served by teaching them options for coping skills and skills for self-advocacy. Awareness about why certain situations or environments might require an adjustment of behavior can be helpful, but agency to determine what is best for themselves should be given.

The benefit of recognizing autism early is that it empowers kids to know and understand themselves, and to learn to self-advocate for the accommodations they need and deserve.

Although we are getting better at recognizing autism, there are still factors that greatly slow the identification of twice-exceptional gifted/autistic kids and teens. One of the first signs of autism when children are young is a lag in developing language skills, however, many twice-exceptional gifted/autistic kids do not experience a language delay. Compensatory skills and masking make it possible that gifted/autistic kids look a little "quirky," but aren't noticeably struggling until social expectations begin to outpace their compensatory abilities. And autistic girls are often the last to be diagnosed because so much of the research and awareness about autism has been focused historically on boys. Autistic girls tend to be more motivated to socialize than boys, so they blend in more easily and their special interests are more closely aligned with what neurotypical kids enjoy (like a certain musical group or other popular trend).

Gifted/autistic children are often extremely talented and if they are able to harness their passions/special interests, they can use them to drive themselves toward success. They often thrive when using logical and critical thinking skills. They tend to lean toward linear thinking and are most successful when expectations along with individual steps are outlined toward a goal, rather than facing ambiguous or unclear expectations.

Pathological Demand Avoidance

A term used to describe a specific set of behaviors and characteristics co-occurring with autistic individuals is pathological demand avoidance (PDA). PDA is more familiar in the UK and Australia, although gradually it is becoming known in the US. It is a profile of the autism spectrum that is characterized by avoidance of everyday demands. The term "pathological" is not neurodiversity-affirming, and many prefer to think of it as pervasive demand avoidance, describing how the pattern impacts the daily lives of PDAers. Many PDAers tend to be bright and are able to mask many of their autistic characteristics easily; they also may be more socially motivated than other autistic people.[7] However, this often masks the fact that a deeper understanding of those social situations is lacking. PDA can often be mistaken for oppositional-defiant disorder (ODD). Anxiety tends to be at the root of demand avoidance for PDAers and working to reduce the anxiety about fulfilling requests is helpful for managing PDA.[8] Chapter 5 discusses specific strategies about communicating with children dealing with pervasive demand avoidance traits.

Specific Learning Disabilities

Gifted students who struggle with academic skills may have a specific learning disability (SLD). Specific learning disabilities include the diagnoses known as dyslexia, dyscalculia, and dysgraphia, although the DSM-5 uses the terminology "specific learning disorder" for the official diagnosis when assessed.[9] Each of these diagnoses is separate from an individual's overall cognitive ability.

Because these types of learning disabilities are independent from overall cognitive skills, it is possible for any gifted child to also have a learning disability. However, it is often difficult for families to secure special education services for these twice-exceptional children because of the compensatory skills 2e kids develop. (Chapter 12 talks about how to advocate for support at school for 2e students with SLDs.)

Just like other types of neurodivergence, specific learning disabilities are based in neurobiological differences of the brains of twice-exceptional kids. While a child may get support to develop reading, writing, or math skills, they aren't "cured" from their learning disability. Accommodations for twice-exceptional kids, including assistive technology, like speech-to-text software or smart notebooks for taking notes, can help mitigate the impact of a learning disability. If parents are seeking support for dyslexia specifically, Orton-Gillingham-based models for remediating reading skills are the most effective method for support. Orton-Gillingham methods are multi-sensory and work to establish new neural pathways associating sounds with letters to assist with reading.

Dyslexia
Dyslexia is a term meaning a child who struggles to connect phonological sounds to the symbols that are used in writing.

This causes trouble with reading fluency and can impact reading comprehension skills. One can also have a diagnosis of specific learning disability in reading comprehension, which is different than dyslexia; typically, twice-exceptional learners are able to comprehend what they read quite well, even if they are unable to fluently read a lot of the text. They often use their deep background knowledge and ability to make inferences based on the parts of a passage or book that they can read, then fill in the blanks. Although many people believe dyslexia is related to writing and reading letters backwards or upside-down, it is not related to a visual processing difficulty. Some dyslexic children may transpose letters because of the difficulty with associating the sounds to letters when sounding words out (for example, /p/ and /b/ are based on the same mouth movements, but one is "voiced" and the other is not; this can lead to confusion when trying to sound out and spell words for dyslexic students).

Dysgraphia

Dysgraphia is when someone struggles with writing, specifically in areas like spelling and handwriting. Difficulty with spacing and forming letters, writing grammatically correct sentences, and writing complete words without skipping letters are all signs of dysgraphia. Trouble with expressing one's thoughts in words in writing doesn't technically fall under the label of dysgraphia; this type of difficulty is known as a specific learning disorder in written expression. Disorganized essays, words that are misused, and written work that seems incomplete can each be signs of an SLD in written expression.

Dyscalculia

Dyscalculia impacts someone's ability to learn and apply number-related concepts, like basic mathematical operations or mathematical reasoning. Some signs that a child is struggling with dyscalculia might be difficulty with sequencing items or understanding the concepts of quantities, like first and last or largest and smallest. Memorizing math facts can be tricky for kids with dyscalculia. Counting money and estimating time are also areas where dyscalculia can impact someone.

Processing Disorders

Processing disorders, like central auditory processing disorder (CAPD), visual processing disorder (VPD), and sensory processing disorders (SPD) can also impact twice-exceptional learners. Each of these diagnoses influences how information is received and interpreted in the brain. CAPD is a medical diagnosis recognized by the medical community, while VPD and SPD are terms used to describe a cluster of symptoms that are generally sub-diagnostic and may or may not align with another diagnosis. This means that if a family is trying to receive services such as a Section 504 plan (see Chapter 13) for accommodations, CAPD is likely the only one of the three that will be able to be documented and used for this type of support. (Some schools may provide more leeway based on how significantly a child is impacted by the processing issues.) Processing disorders are frequently found with a co-occurring diagnosis, often also associated with neurodiversity.

Central Auditory Processing Disorder

CAPD occurs when a student is able to hear with no physical concerns, but they may have a hard time differentiating voices from background noise. Some people with CAPD describe taking additional time to sort through the sounds in a conversation with multiple people, and by the time they've interpreted what was said and come up with their response, the conversation has already moved on. CAPD is typically diagnosed by an audiologist.

Visual Processing Disorder

VPD can impact a child's ability related to hand–eye coordination or reading and writing. Some individuals with VPD may benefit from vision therapy. Vision therapy can identify specific problems with visual processing, such as eye teaming (the eyes both lining up to follow a point of focus) and eye tracking (shifting smoothly from focusing on one object to another). Vision therapy has been developed to work on these particular skills.

Sensory Processing Disorder

SPD involves sensory processing difficulties. Table 3.1 earlier in this chapter provides examples of each of the types of sensitivity that can occur with sensory processing concerns. Occupational therapy can be a resource for kids who struggle with sensory processing; during occupational therapy, they can learn strategies to reduce sensitivities or ways to regulate their sensory needs in order to lessen their impact in daily life.

Anxiety- and Depression-Based Diagnoses

When we start discussing anxiety- and mood-related diagnoses, the line for where neurodiversity ends and mental health diagnoses begin starts to get very blurred. Obsessive-compulsive disorder (OCD) and bipolar are frequently labeled as types of neurodivergence, while generalized anxiety disorder (GAD) and major depressive disorder (MDD) fall under the umbrella of mental health/illness. Other types of related diagnoses straddle that line: for example, social anxiety disorder (SAD) is an anxiety-based psychological diagnosis that frequently co-occurs with autism; it isn't really the same as GAD which often has a specific environmental trigger, but it isn't really a type of neurodivergence on its own, either. For the purposes of this book, we are going to consider gifted kids and teens who experience any of the above diagnoses as twice-exceptional because they each influence how they are able to perform academically, manage their emotions, and interact with others. Additionally, when we are working to support our kids who have one or more of these diagnoses, we can continue to leverage their strengths based on their cognitive ability to help support them.

Generalized Anxiety Disorder

Characterized by intense and pervasive worry, GAD can cause kids and teens to feel unnecessary stress. Gifted kids who experience GAD may appear perfectionistic and become preoccupied with their grades. Because gifted kids have advanced verbal abilities, they may be more aware of things that are happening in the world around them compared to their peers. Without the life experience behind them to contextualize these situations, they may become overly fearful and anxious about situations beyond their control. Irritability and low tolerance for frustration are some outward signs of anxiety in kids and teens, as well as difficulty concentrating or sleeping.

Social Anxiety Disorder

Fear of being judged or being caught in an awkward situation with no escape can cause kids and teens with SAD to avoid social situations, even when they would like to participate. If a child only becomes socially anxious around adults, but is comfortable around peers, they typically don't meet the criteria necessary for a diagnosis of SAD. Another manifestation of SAD that may impact gifted kids and teens is extreme test anxiety; more than being fearful of doing poorly on a test, test anxiety is often related to the fear of judgment when the assessment is graded.

Obsessive-Compulsive Disorder

OCD is characterized by obsessive thoughts, which are intrusive and unwanted, and compulsions, which are urges to complete a behavior to alleviate the fear or stress associated with the obsessive thought. There are multiple types of presentations of OCD. Some that are most often seen in children:

- ◆ Fear of contamination – intense fear of getting sick, touching things that might be dirty, or germs. COVID both triggered and exacerbated OCD symptoms for some kids, which is the most common type of OCD among children.
- ◆ Looking for things to be "just right" – driven by a desire to do something until they get the "right feeling" or the activity has been done "just right." This leads to doing things over and over until they feel like it was done correctly, even if they can't identify what specifically makes it correct or incorrect. This might look like perfectionism on overdrive if it impacts a child in an academic setting.

◆ Magical thinking – fear that if something isn't done in a particular way, something bad will happen. Sometimes the rituals completed to avoid the bad thing from happening include patterns of numbers (doing something a certain number of times, for example) or having to walk in a certain path to get from class to class.

◆ Aggressive obsessions – repeated thoughts about bad things they can do can cause significant distress. They may be afraid of hurting another person or themselves, even if they don't want to do so.

Major Depression

Kids who are dealing with depression might appear to have increased tearfulness, irritability, changes in sleeping and eating patterns, and a loss of interest in activities that used to be enjoyable. They may verbalize thoughts of death or suicide. Noting these apparent changes in behavior and speaking directly to kids about how they are doing is necessary to support them. At school, kids dealing with depression might need accommodations or extended time for assignments. Counseling is also helpful to develop coping skills to manage depression.

If you are concerned that your child is thinking about harming themselves in any way, don't be afraid to ask directly about whether or not those thoughts are on their mind. Ask these questions: Are they thinking about death or dying? Have they thought about how they would try to hurt themselves (and, if so, how the would do so)? Do they plan to take action on the thoughts of hurting themselves? These questions can be hard to ask and hearing the answers even harder, but ultimately, knowing is better than not because it can allow you to get your child the help they need. If your child is engaging in self-injury, but they are not suicidal, try to ask questions to understand. Non-suicidal self-injury is a concern to be addressed from a place of support, without causing additional shame or fear of being discovered.

Some gifted kids may have questions about topics related to existence in general about topics like existential isolation, freedom, meaninglessness, and death. While these questions can be associated with "existential depression," this isn't necessarily the same as clinical depression. Be cautious and supportive to help kids answer these questions within the context of their lived experiences, but don't be alarmed when and if these questions arise.

Other Types of Twice-Exceptionality

There are many other diagnoses that a gifted individual can experience, requiring additional support at home and school. These types of twice-exceptionality are either not as common as the diagnoses already mentioned, or align closely or co-occur with them.

Bipolar

Bipolar disorder typically begins to show symptoms in late adolescence and early adulthood, although children are rarely diagnosed with it. Bipolar I is characterized by symptoms aligning with a major depressive disorder and alternating with at least one experience of mania (a period with a specific onset and end of persistent and unusual elevated mood). Bipolar is much more impactful than abrupt mood swings through the day, and an experience of mania typically lasts a minimum of one full week. Bipolar II is similar, however, the mania isn't quite as elevated; in this diagnosis, it is referred to as hypomania.

Disruptive Mood Dysregulation Disorder and Oppositional Defiant Disorder

Children who struggle with intense temper outbursts several times a week may qualify for a diagnosis of disruptive mood dysregulation disorder (DMDD). DMDD falls under the category of depressive diagnoses. Children who struggle with argumentative and defiant behaviors may qualify for a diagnosis of oppositional defiant disorder (ODD).

Neither of these diagnoses fits the description of "neurodiversity-affirming." They describe problematic behavior, but don't address the underlying cause. For example, a child with DMDD or ODD could also be autistic or an ADHDer, either of which could cause the emotional dysregulation. An autistic child with a PDA profile can easily be mistaken for ODD or an ADHDer with significant rejection sensitivity might look like they fit the diagnosis for DMDD. Slapping on a label of DMDD or ODD is rarely useful because it doesn't work to explain the factors that are influencing the behaviors or provide any specific ideas and interventions. There is some evidence that DMDD may be present in children who are eventually diagnosed with bipolar and a better diagnosis for them, however, this is not yet agreed upon in the field of psychiatry.[10] If there is a benefit to having one of these labels in addition to another diagnosis because it provides additional services or support, they can be helpful; however, families are encouraged to be cautious if it is offered as a standalone diagnosis.

Selective/Situational Mutism

Listed as an anxiety-based diagnosis, selective mutism (SM) is described as an inability to speak in certain social situations where speaking is expected, although speaking in other situations is not problematic. Neurodiversity-affirming advocates prefer to use the term "situational mutism" instead of "selective mutism," which recognizes the impact of the environment in causing anxiety-induced mutism, instead of a selection that is consciously made by an individual. Children who are autistic or have significant social anxiety may exhibit traits of SM. Supporting kids with selective mutism relies heavily on relationship building, trust, and establishing an environment that feels safe so a child is able to risk speaking in situations they find overwhelming. It is common that a child with selective mutism speaks freely while at home with their immediate family, but is unable to speak in other social situations or when other people are present.

Tourette's Syndrome

Tourette's syndrome is a diagnosis characterized by sudden, recurrent, nonrhythmic motor movements or vocalizations (like humming, throat clearing, or spoken words). Tourette's frequently co-occurs with ADHD, autism, or OCD. Tourette's also causes kids to experience increased anxiety due to worries about engaging in tics in social situations. Tics can interfere with a child's ability to learn and think while in an educational setting, so gifted kids with Tourette's may need accommodations both for how they are assessed for gifted education services and how they are accommodated in the gifted and general education classroom.

Physical disabilities

Gifted children who experience physical disabilities may also require unique accommodations and support at school. For example, the way they are tested for gifted education services may need to be modified in order to accommodate their needs. Twice-exceptional children with physical disabilities may include individuals who are visually impaired, hard of hearing, deaf, or have cerebral palsy, to name a few. Many of these students may already be accessing special education services, and parents of bright kids should advocate for information from special education service providers to be shared with gifted education facilitators, if their ability appears to indicate they would be a good fit for advanced learning opportunities.

Diagnosing Twice-Exceptional Learners

A lot of families arrive in my office because their very bright child is struggling with emotional regulation, mood, or motivation. If it appears there may be another exceptionality present, I start asking questions. Has anyone suggested the possibility of autism? Are they familiar with how ADHD might manifest in a gifted child?

There isn't necessarily a right or wrong answer about whether you should formalize a diagnosis or how and when you should do so. Going through an assessment process can be arduous and expensive process; however, a diagnostic assessment is a prerequisite for accessing many educational services and accommodations or receiving medication. Additionally, there can be value to having your child understand their neurodivergence.

One of the major factors that holds families back from formalizing a diagnosis is the fear that a child who is labeled as neurodivergent will have limited future opportunities. What if the school won't allow them to participate in gifted or honors-level classes? Or they want to apply to a selective high school? Will it impact their college opportunities? In many ways, a diagnosis actually *protects* the child from having limited opportunities. A child who is "just" a behavior problem is going to be much more limited than a child who needs behavioral accommodations due to their diagnosis of ADHD. A child who struggles academically due to dyslexia is entitled to supports to take the coursework that is cognitively challenging for them, but a struggling student without a label might be blocked from accessing those courses. As an added protection, it is illegal for transcripts shared with post-secondary schools to include any information about a student's disability or accommodations.[11]

In almost all cases, finding an accurate diagnosis is a benefit. It provides a starting point to better understand your child and a road map to understand how to support both their abilities and difficulties. Additionally, as advocates for neurodiversity working to reduce the stigma of diagnosis and making the world a more inclusive place, normalizing diagnosis is a key component of this mission.

Medical versus Educational Diagnoses

This chapter specifically addresses the process for seeking a diagnosis through the medical field for your child. Educational diagnoses are covered in more depth in Part IV: Finding the Right Academic Fit. It is important to clarify the difference because twice-exceptional children straddle the worlds of medical and educational diagnoses frequently.

One of the most confounding and confusing aspects of diagnosis for twice-exceptional learners is the fact that a diagnosis from the medical community doesn't guarantee educational services or support, and an educational diagnosis occasionally means a child won't meet criteria for a medical diagnosis. When a parent receives a diagnosis from a medical professional and the school says they can't provide services, it is frustrating, and families are often left feeling helpless.

Medical diagnosis	Educational diagnosis
Provided by a medical professional such as a psychologist, psychiatrist, neuropsychologist, neurologist, primary care physician, or mental health practitioner	Provided by a team through the schools; team often consists of special education teachers, school psychologists, school psychological examiners, speech–language pathologist, counselors, school administrators, or others
May lead to accommodations and modifications at school through a Section 504 Plan	Generally used to determine special education services through an Individualized Education Plan (IEP)
Diagnosis based on *Diagnostic and Statistical Manual of Mental Disorders* (DSM-5) published by the American Psychiatric Association	Diagnosis based on Individuals with Disabilities Education Act (IDEA) through the US Department of Education

TABLE 3.2 Differences between medical and educational diagnoses

It may be easier for families to access assessment through the medical community than the schools. The process for assessments at school is often influenced by how significantly a student is impacted academically or behaviorally during the school day; many twice-exceptional students' struggles don't manifest significantly enough in the school setting to move the assessment process forward. Of course, the cost of a full psychological assessment outside of the schools can vary drastically based on insurance coverage and geography.

It is important for advocates to know the right language to use and how nuances between the medical and educational diagnoses might influence your ability to access services for your child. Table 3.2 explains some of the differences between medical and educational diagnoses.

Finding the Right Professional for Assessments

It is disheartening to see the number of twice-exceptional clients who arrive at my office with an incorrect diagnosis because their cognitive ability wasn't considered during their assessment.

Navigating the medical field and finding the best professional to assess your twice-exceptional child can be trickier than
it seems. Finding a practitioner who understands how giftedness
can influence and interact with other types of neurodivergence
is key, and, unfortunately, many in the medical field are unaware
of how to interpret test results when cognitive giftedness is also
present. What should parents look for to make sure they find an
accurate diagnosis?

Is Giftedness Considered?

If you can't find a professional in your area who specifically states
they provide assessments for twice-exceptional children, you can
start by asking questions about how the clinician uses cognitive
ability within the diagnostic process. Twice-exceptional kids
develop many coping skills to compensate for their struggles.
Additionally, the cutoff scores for meeting diagnostic thresholds
are based on populations of children whose intelligence follows
the same distribution of IQ as the general population. This means
only a very small percentage of individuals included in the process of creating an assessment were gifted; this can lead to 2e kids
with compensatory skills having scores that are "sub-diagnostic"
when compared to other children their age.

University of Iowa's Belin-Blank Center is home to
Dr. Megan Foley-Nicpon, who was a guest on episode 44 of *The
Neurodiversity Podcast*. She shared about the importance of contextualizing assessment results with cognitive ability. She gave
several examples of how giftedness can influence the outcome of
certain types of screeners and assessments, including one about
how they studied whether or not autism screeners were capable
of catching gifted students who had previously been diagnosed
with autism.

> We looked at a group of gifted individuals who were
> diagnosed with autism spectrum disorder. ... We then
> gave those youth screening instruments to see whether or
> not they would still be diagnosed with autism, and they
> all weren't [although] they all should have been, because

this was a screening instrument. So, it said to us that these screeners may not capture the gifted student with autism traits in order to recommend whether or not they should receive a full evaluation.[12]

Is a Differential Diagnosis Process Followed?

Best practice for identifying twice-exceptional learners involves conducting what is called a differential diagnosis. A differential diagnosis is generally completed by a clinical psychologist or neuropsychologist and involves an assessment that looks at *everything* and attempts to rule things out. The benefit to conducting the assessment with this method is that it reduces the chance of ending up with an inaccurate result.

When completing a differential diagnosis, clinicians who are trained in psychological assessments develop a specific and thorough plan for each individual. A full assessment that provides a differential diagnosis typically includes a cognitive assessment (IQ), achievement tests (academics), and multiple social, emotional, or behavioral scales. Depending on the areas of concern, a computerized continuous performance test (inattention and impulsiveness), various speech or language assessments (expressive, receptive, and pragmatic language skills), or observational assessments may be included. A thorough and detailed patient history is also gathered. All of this information is assimilated to identify and confirm an accurate diagnosis.

A differential diagnosis method is the most thorough way to assess 2e learners and helps avoid a misdiagnosis (false positive) or missed diagnosis (false negative). Dr. Catherine Hasler is a clinical psychologist who described the reasons why a differential diagnosis is important for accurate diagnosis for twice-exceptional children on episode 17 of *The Neurodiversity Podcast*. "A differential diagnosis allows us to presume nothing when they come in about a specific diagnosis. Sometimes people kind of latch on to a certain symptom or maybe somebody else has suggested something. … It's kind of confirmation bias. They look for those pieces that fit with that without looking at everything else."[13]

A Needle in a Haystack

You've googled, asked the gifted specialist and counselor at the school, and crowd-sourced members of 2e parenting social media groups. If you've been able to find a clinician who specializes in twice-exceptionality, is close to your home, and takes your insurance, you should immediately go and purchase a lottery ticket. For those of you who still are stuck, don't give up.

When you find a clinician who seems like they might be a good fit, ask some questions. (If at all possible, ask them directly, perhaps during an intake appointment or prior to scheduling the assessment.) People in the field of psychology generally want to help and understand their clients and may be willing to learn in order to make sure they come to an accurate diagnosis. Some questions you may want to ask include:

◆ Are you familiar with the term twice-exceptional?
◆ Do you complete a differential diagnostic process? How do you determine what assessments to use?
◆ How do you take cognitive ability into account when completing assessments and making a diagnosis?
◆ Have you seen other patients who have a diagnosis of dyslexia/autism/ADHD and were also gifted? If so, how did being gifted influence that diagnosis?

Misdiagnosis and Missed Diagnosis

There is a lot of talk in the field of gifted development about the risks of misdiagnosis or missed diagnosis. Some of the possible barriers to accurately diagnosing twice-exceptional children include:

◆ Twice-exceptionality is misunderstood, and a wrong diagnosis is given (for example, an ADHD diagnosis is given when autism is the accurate diagnosis).
◆ A diagnosis is missed because gifted characteristics mask the difficulties.

◆ A lack of familiarity with twice-exceptionality leads to assessments being interpreted incorrectly (for example, missing dyslexia because the child is considered "at grade level").
◆ Concerns are explained away and minimized as "gifted quirkiness" without investigation.
◆ Giftedness is pathologized and a diagnosis is given when no diagnosis is appropriate.

Some parents and professionals fear that gifted children will be misdiagnosed because the characteristics of their giftedness are misinterpreted as a symptom of another label. While this is possible, the existence of a wrong diagnosis or a missed diagnosis should also be considered. Each of these can have lasting impacts ranging from accessibility of services, lost time for proactive interventions, and the impact of internalized experiences for an inaccurately diagnosed child.

Should We Use Medication?

Depending on the diagnosis your child receives, you may have the option of trying medication as one tool to help your child. Choosing whether to use medication to mitigate a child's difficulties is one of the hardest choices a parent can make. As adults, when we choose to take a medicine, we are attuned to how we feel, if it is working, and if there are any side effects. Giving medication to our children is a different story. Kids aren't great at noticing the subtle changes the medication might have. And, of course, nobody wants to take unnecessary medication.

When I'm working with families at the office and they are faced with the decision to try medication or not, we usually take a cautious step-by-step approach and choose medication after other options have been utilized and aren't as effective as we'd hoped. Through counseling, we work to develop different strategies and coping skills to improve overall functioning. We implement structures and accommodations at home and school to reduce the impact of the diagnosis. But, finally, if there are struggles we're still not able to manage, I encourage families to talk to their doctors about medication.

As with any decision, whether or not to try medication comes down to weighing the benefits compared to the drawbacks. Consider the self-beliefs your child is adopting while they are struggling. Do they think they are lazy? That they are a bad kid? That they are dumb? What if medication was the small tool necessary to prevent those internalized beliefs?

Sometimes kids are hesitant to try medication or feel like they "should" be able to manage their difficulties on their own. I like to talk to kids about how their brains are wired and how the medication works to help. I ask them to visualize what their life would be like if they weren't constantly feeling overwhelmed by stress, social anxiety, or disorganization. How much would they be able to do? How much success would they achieve? What would that big exhale of relief really feel like?

One last thought if you think medication might help but you are worried about trying it: If it doesn't work or you don't like the side effects, you can stop giving your child the medication. It is easy to forget that just because a decision is made once doesn't mean it is made forever. Your doctor will advise you on how to stop the medication.

Should I Tell My Child about Their Diagnosis?

Sometimes parents ask *if* they should tell their child about their neurodivergence, although I know what they really mean is *when* should they tell their child about their diagnosis. Some parents are concerned their child will think there is something wrong with them if they have a diagnosis; others worry their bright children will latch onto the label as an excuse to avoid effort in their areas of difficulty.

Neurodivergent kids know they are different. They recognize that they experience the world differently than their peers.

They know the effort they put forth in class, social situations, or staying organized is more than what their peers expend; they also feel the discrepancy between the things that come easily to them and those that don't. Being open and honest about their unique learning profile is necessary to build the skills they will need for success: self-advocacy, emotional regulation, and executive functioning skills. Pretending areas of difficulty don't exist leads to shame, embarrassment, and loss of motivation. Chapter 4 discusses specific ideas about how to have this conversation with your child.

There are times when our bright kids begin to invoke the name of their disability as a way to avoid accountability or effort when things get hard. Parents and teachers are often worried they will develop a sense of learned helplessness. I recognize this concern; however, I also think we might be misplacing our fear. Our kids are going to try to find excuses for all kinds of situations. How we help them push through those excuses isn't reliant on whether or not we told them about their twice-exceptionality. I frequently talk with kids about how knowledge is power, and because they have this information about themselves, it actually gives them *less* of an excuse because by knowing exactly what their difficulties are, it gives them the opportunity to build those skills or find ways to overcome them.

The Long-Term Impact of Being Undiagnosed

Many twice-exceptional adults can tell you first-hand about the long-term impact of being undiagnosed and unsupported. The neurodiverse community is full of stories of late-diagnosed twice-exceptional people who never received the accommodations or tools they needed when they were young. They talk about being misunderstood for years and the liberation of finally having a new level of self-awareness; they also talk about the impact of having been unsupported while younger, not having the terminology to express their needs or self-advocate. I have an (untested and generally unscientific) hypothesis that a high percentage of people who relate to the "gifted kid burnout" meme are essentially undiagnosed twice-exceptional adults.

In the field of psychology, we're learning more about trauma and the body's and mind's reaction to traumatic experiences. There is big-T Trauma (major events like natural disasters or acts of violence) and little-t trauma (events that are often chronic or repeated, having long-term effects, like bullying or neglect). Some experiences with unsupported twice-exceptionality can fit into the little-t trauma category.

Julian was a second-grade student I worked with. He had been identified as gifted at his school but was having significant behavioral issues at school. His teachers described him as disrespectful; at times, he became so dysregulated he would melt down and the other students would have to leave the classroom because his behavior became destructive, throwing things and ripping up papers. He was undiagnosed autistic and dealing with demand avoidance. His social communication difficulties were masked by his giftedness; his honest queries to the teacher were interpreted as challenging authority (he *really* didn't understand the expectations). His rigid thinking led to perfectionism and shutting down if he made a mistake. Instead of providing supports through accommodations or special education services, the school wanted to handle everything as a disciplinary issue and assess him for a conduct disorder.

Liana was identified for gifted education services as a fourth grader through her school's universal screening process. Liana was undiagnosed dyslexic and was extremely anxious in social situations. This meant reading aloud was panic inducing. One expectation in her gifted education classroom was to read above-level books in small groups and participate in book club style conversations about the books. After a semester of terrifying experiences where her teacher insisted she share in front of a group about a book she could barely read and understand, Liana dropped the gifted program. The students tormented her with jokes about how she faked her way into the gifted program and then couldn't cut it.

For Julian, the lasting impact of going through school with fear of getting in trouble for behavior led him to drop out of high school. Liana's anxiety grew to a point that she began refusing to go to school; her parents eventually chose to homeschool her, which is when they finally discovered her dyslexia.

While each of these examples is extreme both in the lack of support offered when the difficulties arose and the ultimate outcome experienced, the lasting effect of chronically feeling stressed and unsuccessful in the academic setting for many twice-exceptional kids is real. Each of these students endured negative experiences that could have been mitigated with appropriate diagnosis and accommodations. We need to ask ourselves: How can we provide an intellectually safe environment for our twice-exceptional kids?

Chapter Reflection

- ◆ How has your child's diagnosis impacted how you relate to their achievement or behavior?
- ◆ What language do you use when talking about labels with your child? How have they responded to understanding or knowing about their diagnoses or identification(s)?
- ◆ How did your child's cognitive ability influence your ability to get a diagnosis, or how did your child's diagnosis impact their identification as gifted?
- ◆ Parents describe a wide range of what prompted them to seek a diagnosis for their child. What shaped your decision to seek or hold off on finding a diagnosis for your child? If you've been through this process, what are your feelings about it?
- ◆ Are you aware of anyone who grew up with an undiagnosed exceptionality? (Maybe it was you?) How has that influenced their adult life?
- ◆ What are your feelings about disclosing your child's diagnosis to them? What factors play into these emotions?

Notes

1. Rinn, A. N. (2020). *Social, emotional, and psychosocial development of gifted and talented individuals*. Waco, TX: Prufrock Press.

2. Robison, J. E. (2013, October 7). What is neurodiversity? [Web log post]. Retrieved from https://www.psychologytoday.com/us/blog/my-life-aspergers/201310/what-is-neurodiversity

3. Davis, J. L. (2020, July 22). Twice-exceptionality + cultural diversity = 3e [Audio blog interview]. Retrieved from https://neurodiversitypodcast.com/home/2020/7/22/episode-63-twice-exceptionality-cultural-diversity-3e

4. Dai, D. Y. (2018). A history of giftedness: a century of quest for identity. In *APA handbook of giftedness and talent* (pp. 3–23). Washington, DC: American Psychological Association.

5. Fugate, M., Gentry, M., & Zentall, S. S. (2014). Creativity and working memory in gifted students with and without characteristics of attention deficit hyperactivity disorder: Lifting the mask. *Gifted Child Quarterly, 57*, 234–236.

6. Babinski, D. E., Kujawa, A., Kessel, E. M., Arfer, K. B., & Klein, D. N. (2018). Sensitivity to peer feedback in young adolescents with symptoms of ADHD: Examination of neurophysiological and self-report measures. *Journal of Abnormal Child Psychology, 47*(4), 605–617. doi:10.1007/s10802–018–0470–2

7. O'Nions, E., Viding, E., Greven, C. U., Ronald, A., & Happé, F. (2013). Pathological demand avoidance: Exploring the behavioural profile. *Autism, 18*(5), 538–544. doi:10.1177/1362361313481861

8. O'Nions, E., Viding, E., Floyd, C., Quinlan, E., Pidgeon, C., Gould, J., & Happé, F. (2017). Dimensions of difficulty in children reported to have an autism spectrum diagnosis and features of extreme/'pathological' demand avoidance. *Child and Adolescent Mental Health, 23*(3), 220–227. doi:10.1111/camh.12242

9. *Diagnostic and statistical manual of mental disorders: DSM-5*. (2017). Arlington, VA: American Psychiatric Association.

10. Alghamdi, W. A. (2021). Disruptive mood dysregulation disorder and its impact on rates of bipolar disorder among children and adolescents. *Current Psychiatry Research and Reviews, 16*(3), 154–157. doi:10.2174/2666082216999200909113835

11. Monroe, S. J. (2008). *Dear colleague letter: Report cards and transcripts for students with disabilities* (United States, Department of Education, Office for Civil Rights).

12. Foley-Nicpon, M. (2019, October 16). Accurate assessment for twice-exceptional kids [Audio blog interview]. Retrieved from https://neurodiversitypodcast.com/home/2019/10/16/episode-44-accurate-assessment-for-twice-exceptional-kids

13. Hasler, C. (2018, September 5). The case for differential diagnosis [Audio blog interview]. Retrieved from https://neurodiversitypodcast.com/home/2018/9/5/episode-17-the-case-for-differential-diagnosis

PART

II

Parent Toolkit

Part II of this book discusses the tools you'll need as a parent to implement the suggested strategies in Part III. The major theme within each chapter is related to communication in some way: How do we communicate and connect with our twice-exceptional kids so we can then help to facilitate their growth and independence? How do we talk to other people in our lives about our child's needs? And how do we talk to our parenting partners and work together effectively to support our child?

DOI: 10.4324/9781003237532-6

4

Talking about Twice-Exceptionality

Parents have many types of reactions and emotions about talking to their children about being twice-exceptional. Often, many of those emotions are tied up with their own feelings about the diagnosis. Will their child interpret the information as something being wrong with them? Will they use the diagnosis as an excuse to reduce their effort on overcoming difficulties? Are they mature enough to understand what it all means?

Let's start with what most would consider an easier conversation: Families may feel uncertain how to talk to their child about being identified as gifted. They may want to prevent their child from feeling different or they may worry it will become fodder for an overgrown ego. It might be more difficult to hide this label if your child is invited to participate in a gifted program than if they've received an individual diagnosis provided outside of the school. Generally, gifted kids know there is something different before anyone has to tell them, and handling that conversation in a matter-of-fact and straightforward way is the best course of action. Framing giftedness as a "not better than or less than, just different from" type of neurodivergence is a good starting point. "Your brain learns differently and sometimes

DOI: 10.4324/9781003237532-7

faster than the other kids your age so your teachers might need to find some different ways to present the information you're supposed to learn so it is the best fit for how your brain grows."

There's no reason not to handle conversations about your child's other exceptionality in the same way. Be matter-of-fact, highlighting both strengths and struggles. "The testing that we did shows that your brain works a little differently. Dyslexia means that the pathways in your brain that help you to read are wired a little differently; it means connecting sounds to letters is a little tricky even though you have great understanding of what the words mean. Dyslexic brains also are known for their creativity."

Here are some tips on how to talk to your child about their diagnosis.

1. Be aware of your own emotions about your child's diagnosis and needs.
2. Facilitate a matter-of-fact conversation about being twice-exceptional. Focus on both the strengths and struggles.
3. Encourage your child to ask questions. Research together if you don't know the answer.
4. Consider using some of the following questions to deepen the conversation, depending on your child's interest and ability.

   a. Have you heard of these terms/diagnoses before? What do you know about them?
   b. In what ways do you think you fit into these characteristics? Are there some that fit and some that don't?
   c. What thoughts/emotions do you have about knowing you are twice-exceptional?
   d. What can we do at home and school right now that might be helpful to you?
   e. Create an "Opportunities and Obstacles" Venn diagram or T-chart together to explore the benefits and drawbacks of twice-exceptionality.

5. Pause the conversation at the end and remind your child that this is a conversation that will keep going. They can bring it up anytime they feel it would be helpful.

As your child gets older, the conversation surrounding twice-exceptionality will evolve. They'll have more questions and more self-awareness of how it impacts them. Neurodiversity-affirming families will encourage these conversations and normalize the fact that some people's brains work differently than others.

Opportunities and Obstacles

Taking the time to reflect on individual strengths and areas for growth can be a part of the conversation you have with your child. Brainstorm the pros and cons with them, listing the areas of twice-exceptionality that are a benefit and the areas that are more difficult. You could also create a Venn diagram because there may be some factors that go in the middle, that have both benefits and drawbacks.

Sharing about Twice-Exceptionality with Family and Friends

Talking to family and friends about twice-exceptionality can be tricky. There are so many prejudices and stereotypes about neurodiversity, it can be like navigating a minefield. "Are you bragging about your kid being gifted?" "If they're so smart, why do they act that way?" "Why would you want your kid in the gifted program if they are dyslexic?" The lack of awareness surrounding neurodiversity combined with the fact that only a small percentage of the world is neurodivergent makes it difficult to find a safe space to talk about your concerns and commiserate with other parents. Many people will want to share their opinion or ideas.

Determining who you'd like to know about your child's diagnosis is a decision you and your child should make together. You can choose to empower your child to have some control over who is given the information about their neurodivergence by asking their permission before sharing. This autonomy has less to do with whether the other person knows about their twice-exceptionality and more to do with your relationship with your child. Involving them in the decision about who receives this privileged information makes them an active participant in their own lives and encourages healthy boundaries and self-advocacy.

If your child struggles in social situations due to social anxiety, lagging social skills, or impulsive behavior, but masks well enough that people also see how bright they are, it is possible you'll be on the receiving end of judgmental commentary of your poor parenting skills. Brace yourself, let it slide, and take a moment to educate the offending person about neurodiversity and the trauma an entire generation of neurodivergent folks experienced by having their differences disciplined out of them. (Okay, maybe decide on the lecture part on a case-by-case basis.)

You may have close family and friends who struggle to understand your child's needs, however, you are in a position where you are required to be around them on certain occasions, like holidays or other events. Parents have shared with me some horror stories of conversations about trying to explain their child's needs. From suggesting disproven theories as cause and solution for neurodivergent struggles to offering to pray so a higher power might remove the "affliction" from the child, these well-meaning but extremely misguided attempts can leave parents of 2e kids feeling angry, discouraged, and isolated.

When you find yourself advocating for your child with close family members and friends, you are also advocating for yourself. Ask yourself what it is that you need from those who are close to you and let them know how they can support you and your child through understanding and compassion.

I wish I had the solution to handing some of the more difficult relationships and conversations. It is easy to suggest ideas. Set clear boundaries! Provide information! Don't take it personally! However, I know most of these relationships have a lot more history and don't exist in a vacuum. The bottom line: You know your child and you know what they need. Try to give these folks the benefit of the doubt that they are attempting to help with whatever resources and information they have available.

Finding Community

When we're talking about a small community of individuals (and twice-exceptional kids are members of at least two small communities simultaneously), geographic barriers can be extremely limiting. One of the wonderful aspects of technology and social media is the ability to find and connect with others who are sharing your experience. Hearing about others' experiences and getting support from others who've been where you are is a huge part of self-care as a parent. The feeling of universality that community provides can become a touchpoint when it feels like nobody else understands what you are going through to support your 2e child. Knowing that other people have succeeded in accessing services or getting their child through college might give you a sigh of relief.

Jen Merrill offered advice on self-care and the importance of finding community on episode 33 of the podcast.

> I highly recommend pushing past your comfort zone or your introversion, or whatever you need to do, and find others in a similar leaking boat, because we're all trying to bail water, with a cracked styrofoam cup. … Just for starters right there, if you're feeling less alone, that's a relief. The internet has been a great blessing in that respect because before finding [people] online I could count on one hand the number of families I know with gifted kids who would understand.[1]

> Other resources are available, too. There are podcasts and blogs that can provide a more in-depth look at people's experiences with twice-exceptionality. You may be able to find a small support group of six or eight members that meets regularly in person or virtually to offer guidance and support. Parenting a twice-exceptional child doesn't have to be a solo event.

What "They" Say

"They" always have lots of comments about what others "should" be doing. I don't know who gave "them" all this power to make theses pronouncements, but I'm giving you permission to ignore whatever it is.

One last consideration about talking to people about twice-exceptionality is related to how you listen to others. There are a lot of myths and misunderstandings about all types of neurodivergence. There's also an expectation that 2e kids "should" reach milestones according to their overall cognitive ability, but their uneven development is unlikely to align with those benchmarks. Remember that your child is an individual and will master those skills at a rate that is appropriate for them. Focus on individual progress and how far you've come instead of what everyone else says about what your child "should" be able to do. And forget whatever it is that "they" say.

Chapter Reflection

- ◆ What does my child know about being twice-exceptional? Do they need more information?
- ◆ Do the people who are close to my family understand twice-exceptionality? Are they willing to learn? What do I need from the people who are close to me?
- ◆ What connections do I have to the neurodiversity-parenting community? Do I feel fulfilled or should I seek other opportunities to link up with others in similar situations?

Note

1. Merrill, J. (2019, May 29). Note to self – be nice to me [Audio blog interview]. Retrieved from https://neurodiversitypodcast.com/home/2019/5/29/episode-33-note-to-self-be-nice-to-me

5

Communicating for Connection

How much influence do parents hold over their children? How significantly do we really impact their overall development? When I think about the influence of peer relationships, internalized societal messages, and a child's inborn personality, I realize our level of influence is much smaller than we'd like it to be. We can nudge and prod and bribe, but ultimately, our children belong to themselves and we're supporting actors in their lives.

The only area where we truly have the ability to facilitate change is inside our relationship with our children. The well-known psychologist, Carl Rogers, talked about the importance of the therapeutic relationship and how the most important healing part of the relationship between a therapist and their client takes place through the unconditional positive regard a clinician provides to their clients.[1] The same is true for parenting. Our connection with our children is a microcosm of how they will learn to interact with the outside world. As our children grow, they try on various personas. How we react lays the foundation for openness and trust with our children. Do we accept them and validate their attempts to create an identity for themselves? Is it possible as parents to provide structure and support for our children, even when they are engaging in behavior we would prefer for them to stop? How can we let our children know that the

DOI: 10.4324/9781003237532-8

space in our family, within our relationship, is the safest place to figure out exactly who they are?

Our relationship with our children is created through communication – what we say, how we say it, and what our actions show about what we mean. Because the world gives twice-exceptional children so many mixed messages about who they are and who they should be, it is especially important for us to be as consistent with our communication as possible. Understanding our children and ourselves is key to providing this stability.

Communicating for Second-Order Change

Underlying the work we are doing to build connection with our neurodivergent kids is the intent of creating change. We want our kids to be more empowered, independent, and contented in their lives. We want our houses to be calmer and to let down our guard about our children's success at school. We want harmonious relationships that don't rely on power struggles and strategic maneuvering to get things done.

Families in my office share with me all the things they've already tried with their kids – behavior charts, cash for grades, punishments, bribery – and that nothing has worked. They want to know the magic, the one thing that is going to fix all of the difficulties they've had. During sessions, both kids and parents revert to these behaviorist strategies that society has ingrained in us as the only way to facilitate change. But a new behavior chart or a new study strategy – these all might work in the short term, but they are first-order changes. These are changes that occur within the system that already exists, and we already know this system isn't working. We need a new system.

A new system involves second-order change. We need a way to look at things differently and find new solutions. This second-order change involves breaking free from the systems that aren't working and creating something new. For neurodivergent families, this has to start with communication and a collaborative effort between parents and kids.

The changes we need to implement might seem slight, but they are significant. For example, one of the major themes you'll see addressed throughout this book are ways that we can work to shift the power of decision-making and change to our kids. Instead of using a behavior chart to earn a prize at the end of the week, we take the valuable part of this exercise – having a way to monitor and keep track of specific responsibilities – and turn it into a tool that a child uses to self-evaluate and self-regulate their actions. Without a prize or a consequence tied to it, we are transcending the common system that is often oppressive and damaging to relationships. We are facilitating second-order change. Communication that is consistent and solution-focused is the first step to creating this change.

Tools for Communication

There are subtle shifts we can make in how we communicate with our children to offer space for them to solve their own problems. When we allow our kids to solve their own problems, we provide them autonomy and send them the message that we trust them. The first step to facilitating these conversations involves holding back our knee-jerk response to correct, suggest, or solve.

Refraining from judgment during these conversations is key to preventing a relationship where our kids are afraid to tell us things because they think we are going to tell them all the things they are doing wrong. Take some time and observe how you respond when you hear something that elicits a strong emotional response from you. How might the other person perceive your reaction? How will their perception influence what they say or do next? What about the next time they have something to tell you? Will they be inclined to talk to you about it or will they hesitate?

Utilizing a therapeutic mindset as a parent involves keeping a neutral, nonjudgmental reaction to information that is shared. My go-to statements after someone discloses something that catches me off guard in the therapy room are "Wow. I wasn't expecting to hear that," and "Okay. I'm curious to hear more." It is, of course, much easier to keep this stance of neutrality in the counseling office with children who aren't my own. But, even at home, I do my best to push the pause button on my immediate reaction, knowing that my voice and response will greatly influence the course of the conversation and possibly preclude my kids from processing a situation in a way that fosters independence.

Another component of holding onto my judgment in conversations is giving the benefit of the doubt, even when it is clear that I'm being given some elaborations or half-truths. For example, sometimes I'll have clients who share their version of an event that immediately sets off an alarm in my mind that something doesn't add up. Perhaps the story doesn't align with what they've told me in previous sessions, or it directly contradicts what their parents have told me about a situation. If I derail the conversation in order to figure out what is "true," I may lose the opportunity to facilitate change. I might undermine their trust and damage our relationship. But, if I give them the benefit of the doubt and work within the context of what they've shared, we can often work around to the same solutions that we would have otherwise.

For example, your child is talking about a situation at school involving missing work. They are blaming the teacher for not being clear about directions, but you are fairly sure this was an organizational error on your child's part. Rather than directing your focus on your child's shortcomings with organization or immediately contradicting the possibility that their teacher's directions were flawed, start by validating their experience. "Ugh! I know how frustrating that can be when directions aren't clear. Tell me exactly what happened." As they elaborate, listen for opportunities to work accountability into the conversation. Gently suggest ways to shift the conversation to actionable steps: "I wonder what other kids did," or "I wonder if there is a way we can make sure you don't get stuck in this situation again." By facilitating this conversation with a nonjudgmental tone and giving them the benefit of the doubt, we are shepherding them toward solutions that are their own, plus we escape being cast in the role of the villain.

There are other ideas to help facilitate healthy problem-solving conversations with your child. The following list provides some ideas of communication strategies that facilitate nonjudgmental, open conversations:

- ◆ Paraphrasing: Listening to what your child shares with you and simply restating what they've told you in your own words. "It sounds like you're saying ..."
- ◆ Reflection of feeling: Providing a label for the emotion it appears your child is exhibiting.
- ◆ Asking for elaboration: Using a simple "tell me more" to gather more information and encourage sharing.
- ◆ Identifying obstacles: Prompting your child to make observations about what stood in their way related to a particular problem, based on their perception.
- ◆ Wondering: Making comments that present a hypothesis or present a possible alternative perspective.

It is quite easy to fall into the trap of wanting to rescue our kids before they've had the chance to work through a problem on their own. Additionally, it is easy to project your emotions or criticize, especially when there is a role your child has played in the situation that has been addressed in the past. Here are a few common pitfalls that can hinder communication between parents and kids.

- ◆ Invalidating emotions: Contradicting what your child has said or "taking the other side" is a quick way to shut down a child's willingness to share.
- ◆ Reproaching: Expressing disapproval or disappointment for your child's actions.
- ◆ Co-signing: Agreeing with your child's frustration can foster feelings of camaraderie for both you and your child, however, co-signing their complaint doesn't foster autonomy or allow for problem solving.
- ◆ Sidestepping: Focusing on a detail of the situation that isn't the main point for our child and ignoring the disclosure of emotion that was shared.
- ◆ Rescuing: Offering a solution or telling our child what they should do, eliminating their opportunity for autonomy.

Situation	Instead of …	Try …
Your daughter is angry that a teacher won't let her make up a late assignment. She thinks it is because the teacher doesn't like her.	"Of course your teacher likes you!" (*Invalidating emotions*)	"Tell me more about what makes you feel the teacher doesn't like you." (*Paraphrasing, asking for elaboration*)
	"Well, you should have finished your assignment on time." (*Reproaching*)	"I'm curious about the assignment. Was there something that kept it from getting turned in on time?" (*Asking for elaboration, identifying obstacles*)
	"That teacher sounds like he is on a power trip." (*Co-signing*)	"I wonder why the teacher is so firm about those rules." (*Wondering*)
Your son is upset that he isn't allowed to use his phone past a certain time in the evening because he misses texts from his friends, who are allowed to use their phones later.	"Well, that's the rule in our house." (*Sidestepping*)	"I understand the worry about missing out on something with friends." (*Reflecting emotions*)
	"That's ridiculous that your friend's parents let him use his phone all night long." (*Sidestepping*)	"I wonder how different families decide on what works for them." (*Paraphrasing, Wondering*)
Your child is lonely because nobody wants to play the same things they do at recess.	"You shouldn't get stuck on what you want to play; just do what the group wants to do." (*Rescuing*)	"What are the things that they like to play instead?" (*Asking for elaboration*)
	"Well, if you just went along with what everyone else wanted to do, you wouldn't be lonely." (*Invalidating emotions*)	"I wonder what other kids do if everyone wants to play something they aren't interested in doing." (*Wondering*)
Your daughter is embarrassed about having a meltdown during class because she didn't understand an assignment.	"Everyone gets confused sometimes. You shouldn't make a big deal out of it." (*Invalidating emotions*)	"It seems like you feel a lot of pressure to do well all the time." (*Reflection of feeling, paraphrasing*)
	"Why didn't you just ask the teacher?" (*Reproaching*)	"I bet you felt really stuck." (*Reflection of emotion*)

TABLE 5.1 Strategies for avoiding communication pitfalls

Interpreting Neurodivergent Communication

The single most impactful thing a parent can do to help their child is learn how to responsively communicate based on their child's communication style. How do our children best receive our messages? Neurodivergent people often have different communication styles than others, and being aware of the way your child best receives and expresses their thoughts and emotions is the key to supporting them in all environments. Here are some common hurdles twice-exceptional kids might face related to communication.

- ◆ *How does your child react to perceived criticism?* Twice-exceptional children might be especially susceptible to rejection sensitivity. As discussed in Chapter 3, ADHDers have a propensity to be hyperaware of perceived criticism, but other neurodivergent communication styles might also put 2e kids at risk. For example, if a child isn't great at noticing underlying communication cues in social situations, they may misinterpret suggestions or ideas as personal attacks. Or, a twice-exceptional child who has received mixed messages about their school performance or behavior might be wary that any constructive feedback has an underlying malicious intent. While we want to help our children build their resilience to handle these types of situations, we can also help facilitate difficult conversations by noticing when our words could be misinterpreted and providing clear, explicit information.

- ◆ *Does your child need processing time before responding?* In addition to many twice-exceptional kids needing time to think about and consider their responses before responding in general, having conversations where emotions are heightened can increase the amount of time it takes for a 2e kid to put their thoughts into words. It is so easy as a parent to jump into any pause in a conversation and fill in the empty space, or to try to guess what they're thinking. Often the best thing we can do to foster independence and self-advocacy is just wait. Give your child time to really come up with how they want to reply and empower them to find the "just right" words to explain their thoughts and feelings. This might even mean pausing a conversation and returning to it at another time; allowing emotions to settle before forcing a conversation to process a situation might be one of the most productive ways to find a solution. Forcing a conversation before a child is ready likely means they aren't really ready to act on any parts of the conversation yet.

◆ *Does your child have a difficult time talking about their emotions?* Just like the sensitivity to perceived rejection, there are many reasons that twice-exceptional kids might have a hard time talking about their emotions. Some 2e kids might deal with alexithymia – the inability to identify and describe one's emotions – due to a specific type of neurodivergence (especially autistic kids or kids with sensory processing difficulties). Other twice-exceptional kids might have a hard time verbalizing their emotions simply because talking about their emotions requires them to think about the emotions and brings those feelings back to the surface, which can be uncomfortable. Chapter 8 talks specifically about building emotional literacy, which is an important foundational skill in building emotional regulation. Providing processing time and working to build emotional literacy skills are key to helping kids identify and share their emotions.

◆ *Has your child internalized a sense of learned helplessness?* Twice-exceptional kids are prone to developing symptoms of learned helplessness when opportunities for risk-taking and challenge are removed from their paths. There is a fine line between offering accommodations or support and enabling a child who is able to undertake a challenge on their own. During a conversation that is focused on problem solving, learned helplessness can lead a child to shut down or refuse any possible solution that may arise. They may be afraid to risk offering solutions. Working on brainstorming ideas together and allowing your child to take risks on ideas they think are worthwhile is a way to gradually overcome learned helplessness.

What if My Communication Style Doesn't Align with My Child's?

If you are a neurodivergent parent to a neurodivergent kid, you're stuck navigating two communication styles that might not align. Maybe your child processes their feelings externally and you prefer to process things with fewer words. Perhaps you couldn't hide your strong emotions if you tried, but your child gets seriously overwhelmed when emotional situations occur. Think of the two conversation styles like a Venn diagram – where are the overlaps? Are there certain times of day that work best for conversations? Is it easier to communicate in writing through a shared journal or texting rather than having a face-to-face conversation? While it is often true that the apple doesn't fall far from the tree, it is also good to remember that both you and your child's communication styles are valid and worthy of being honored.

The Power of Self-Disclosure

Kids seem to think adults always have everything figured out. When they are young, we are the protectors who watch over them. As they get older, they notice that – in their eyes – we do almost everything well. (I'll never get over how impressed kids are with my pretty basic drawing skills.) Even the most contradictory of teens often believes that adults have the confidence to know how to handle every situation.

Adults sometimes fall into the trap of not wanting kids (or anyone?) to see them struggle. It could be that perfectionism prevents us from showing our areas of weakness. Perhaps emotional intensity prevents us from wanting to talk about uncomfortable feelings and events. Or it could just be that we are used to solving our own problems and moving on. Whatever the reason, it is important for kids to know that we have situations every day that challenge us and that we use specific coping skills to handle them.

There is a fine line with self-disclosure between what is helpful for kids and what is too much. We don't want to put our children in a situation where they are thrust into the role of adult and feel like they need to help us manage our emotions. But, showing our vulnerability and how we handle those uncomfortable emotions is good. There are two ways to use self-disclosure that can be helpful to build connection through communication.

- ◆ *Extemporaneous self-disclosure*: Extemporaneous self-disclosure takes place when we model our thoughts and coping skills in the moment. Often this means verbalizing what we are thinking and feeling as we are experiencing a dysregulating event. For example, imagine you receive an email from work that is asking you to rearrange your schedule for the following day, but you have several events that are not going to be easy to move. Narrate what is going through your head. "Okay, I need to just take a deep breath [*coping strategy*]. I'm feeling really irritated [*labeling emotions*] right now because of this email I got from work [*identifying reason for distress*]. It is stressful to have to change my schedule and I feel worried that the people whose meetings I have to now reschedule will be disappointed in me [*labeling emotions, identifying thoughts about negative outcomes*]. I'm going to sit here for a few minutes and let my heart rate slow down [*identifying physical signs of stress*] and then I'm going to figure out the best way to handle this situation. It is hard for me to handle unexpected changes, but I've had to do it before and it has all worked out [*modeling realistic, solution-focused self-talk*]."
- ◆ *Reflective self-disclosure*: Reflective self-disclosure is another way to build connection with kids and facilitate healthy conversations. It is also a great way to give kids permission to disclose their own difficulties. You might share about a time something embarrassing happened to you to encourage your child to share about an embarrassing experience they are afraid to talk to you about. Or you could share a time you engaged in the same behavior to show you understand the motives for their behavior. For example, say your child is denying their role in a peer dispute at school and is stuck on not admitting (or perhaps doesn't recognize) their error. You might recall a time you had a similar situation occur: "I remember when my friend got really mad at me because I kept saying something over

and over even though they asked me to stop. I actually thought it was funny and that we were just joking around, but then I felt really guilty when she got up and left the lunch table and wouldn't talk to me for the rest of the day. I definitely misinterpreted that situation! I got a little mad that she reacted so strongly, but ultimately, I told her I was sorry and we got back to being friends." This conversation will vary greatly based on the situation, but the main goal is to normalize the experience your child is having and let them know you understand.

Communicating with PDAers

Chapter 3 discussed the subtype profile of pathological/pervasive demand avoidance (PDA) of autistic kids, but many neurodivergent kids may experience demand avoidance for various reasons. The PDA Society suggests using the acronym PANDA to help reduce anxiety and demand avoidance when talking to kids who struggle with overwhelm with the daily expectations of life.[2] Harry Thompson is an autistic PDAer and advocates PDA understanding. He described how the internal experience of a PDAer can be quite different than what it appears externally on episode 54 of *The Neurodiversity Podcast*. "Many parents or teachers might describe the child's meltdown or 'extreme' quote–unquote behavior as an overreaction to simple requests without realizing that the child perceives these requests as inherently dangerous and in some aspects is not able to distinguish a minor request from a genuine threat. So, there's a mismatch of experience worth acknowledging. … We're all reacting accordingly to what we perceive as threats."[3]

While PDA is specific to autistic profiles, demand avoidance in general can be seen in neurodivergent kids based on learned helplessness, burnout, or traumatization from unmet needs. The strategies listed to support PDAers can also be a useful starting point to support any kids (and adults) who are dealing with demand avoidance.

P – Pick battles (allow some choice/control, reduce the number of required rules, explicitly explain reasons/thought patterns for requests, and understand that some things can't be done)

A – Anxiety management (plan for upcoming changes by clearly disclosing plans and eliminating uncertainty, address meltdowns as anxiety-driven, acknowledge sensory and social factors as contributing factors)

N – Negotiation and collaboration (work together to develop a plan to overcome challenges, validate concerns about fairness, establish trusting relationship and rapport prior to negotiation)

D – Disguise and manage demands (frame requests indirectly, work together to complete tasks)

A – Adaptation (give lots of time to complete tasks, be flexible with strategies on how to complete requests, have a backup plan)

Chapter Reflection

♦ How would you describe the communication in your home? When does your family have productive and healthy communication?

♦ How does your neurodivergent child prefer to communicate? Are there situations that hold them back from communicating?

♦ How comfortable are you with using self-disclosure with your child? Are there situations where you think it could be a benefit to use more self-disclosure?

Notes

1. Corey, G. (2021). *Theory and practice of counseling and psychotherapy.* Boston, MA: Cengage.
2. Helpful approaches with PDA – children. (2021, February 13). Retrieved May 01, 2021, from https://www.pdasociety.org.uk/life-with-pda-menu/family-life-intro/helpful-approaches-children/
3. Thompson, H. (2020, March 4). Understanding pathological demand avoidance [Audio blog interview]. Retrieved from https://neurodiversitypodcast.com/home/2020/3/4/episode-54-understanding-pathological-demand-avoidance

6

Effective Co-parenting

Collaborating with another parent on how to raise your child can be difficult. If you are a family that involves step-parents, grandparents, or others who participate in raising your child, it adds exponentially to the difficulty you face. Mix in a little gift-edness and another exceptionality on top of that and it can be quite difficult to make sure everyone is on the same page.

I have a confession: As parents of two confirmed (and one suspected) twice-exceptional kids, one of the few areas where my partner and I find ourselves in disagreements is related to how to parent our kids. Whether it is about how we talk to the kids when we're angry, those split-second discipline decisions ("You're grounded from video games for a year and a half!"), or how much help we should give related to school, we can catch ourselves in heated discussions about the best course of action. Ultimately, I'm grateful to have a partner who is as passionate about supporting our kids as I am.

All the parents I've worked with, without exception, want what is best for their kids. What is "best" is often a matter of opinion, though, and those opinions are informed by a multitude of factors. Our experiences with parents and the educational system from when we were young, our beliefs about human development and personality, and our views on how people change each play a role in how we decide to parent our kids. One of the best things we can do as parents is to try to get out of our own heads and try to focus on our child's needs with an open mind.

DOI: 10.4324/9781003237532-9

Whatever you and your co-parent determine are the best strategies to implement as you work to support your twice-exceptional child, take the time to agree on them and anticipate what this will look like in daily life. Think about discipline, accommodations, and routines. How can things be kept both simple and consistent. In addition to the comfort your child will feel when they know what to expect, it will create a healthy foundation for your co-parenting relationship.

Neurodiversity-Affirming Parenting

The strategies necessary for neurodiversity-affirming parenting presume a few foundational components. Working within this mindset will put you in a place to help facilitate the most growth and change for your twice-exceptional child.

◆ *Parenting is a collaborative process with your child.* There has been a major shift in the understanding of parental roles and relationships, and it is now widely accepted and understood that the healthiest framework for parenting children is with an authoritative parenting style. The three main parenting styles that are commonly cited are authoritarian, authoritative, and permissive. Let's compare parenting styles to learning to drive. An authoritarian parent is going to just do the driving themselves without allowing the child to touch the steering wheel; a permissive parent is going to let their child take the car on a solo joyride before they have their license; and an authoritative parent is somewhere in the middle, sitting in the passenger seat, offering ideas and suggestions, but ultimately letting the child learn by doing. An authoritative parenting style considers a child's autonomy and brings them into the process, letting them know they have an active role in making choices in their life. Striking the balance and hitting the target of authoritative parenting for twice-exceptional kids is important. It values their ability and independence while parents provide structure and support when it is needed.

- *Focus on lagging skills.* The ALSUP (Assessment of Lagging Skills and Unsolved Problems) is a tool created by Dr. Ross Greene.[1] The ALSUP operates under the assumption that children do well if they can, and if they aren't doing well it is because they are lagging behind in the skills necessary to accomplish the task. I first had the opportunity to work with the ALSUP as a school counselor and I've carried this mentality with me since then and use this framework with all of my work with twice-exceptional kids. When we operate from the perspective that all kids want to succeed (they do!) and will do well if they are in an environment that gives them the tools necessary to reach their potential (they will!), we clear the path for growth. We relinquish the constraints of believing our 2e kids should just "try a little harder" or "care a little more."

- *Progress might be slow, but it is still moving forward.* The thing about neurodivergence is that it doesn't go away. An autistic child will be an autistic adult, even if they develop enough coping skills to "pass" as neurotypical. A dyslexic child will always have a dyslexic brain, even if they are able to build the skills so they don't need accommodations any longer. When you start working on the skills that your child needs for success, recognize each success as a step closer to your child's goals. If your child struggles with executive dysfunction or they have a hard time with social communication skills, it is unfair to expect them to magically be able to manage those skills at the same level as their same-age peers because the level of expectations also increases as they get older. It is possible they may never completely "catch up," but remember that catching up isn't necessarily the goal. The goal is to help them learn to work with their strengths and through their struggles. And every little bit of progress is worth celebrating.

What if My Partner Doesn't Agree that Our Child is 2e?

One factor that can be the first to derail supporting your twice-exceptional child is if you and your co-parent(s) don't agree that a diagnosis is valid or necessary. I frequently work with families who have one parent who understands how twice-exceptionality is impacting their child, while the other parent doesn't. Because twice-exceptionality is so often masked and there is significant stigma surrounding many of the diagnoses of neurodiversity, it might be hard for a parent to accept that there is something "wrong" with their child. It might be easier to attribute difficulties to a child's lack of effort or stubbornness; it can be hard to wrap your head around the fact that their difficulties have a neurobiological cause that was possibly influenced by genetics and is therefore not able to be "fixed." Families seeing multiple professionals to identify their child's struggles and receiving different perspectives and diagnoses muddies the waters, and parents might each feel that a different conclusion is the most accurate. Any of the factors that influence the chances of a twice-exceptional child receiving an accurate diagnosis in the first place are possible reasons why parents don't agree on a diagnosis.

Having agreement between parents about the nature of a child's exceptionality is important and is the same reason accurate diagnosis is important in the first place: Diagnosis is the driving force behind supports. What professional resources do we need to access? What is the best way to advocate at the school? How can we best support our child at home? All of these questions are influenced greatly by how we conceptualize a child's exceptionality.

It is possible that you and your co-parent(s) never agree on a diagnosis. Hopefully, finding ways to support your child regardless of diagnosis is manageable. Some parents just take a longer time to understand and accept what having a twice-exceptional child means, and we can give them the time necessary to grow their understanding of it while still providing the support your child needs.

Even parents who are on the same page regarding diagnosis may have a difficult time coming to a consensus about what exactly to do about how to help their child. One parent might lean toward attributing almost all struggles to being twice-exceptional while the other minimizes the impact of neurodivergence and wants the child to try harder. As with most things, the answer likely falls somewhere in the middle. Whenever I have parents who come to my office with this type of disagreement, I'm thrilled because it means they are each in a place where they are working to understand and support their child. If we can all agree that a child needs support, we can get to work. Through time and support, the entire family will be able to see progress that is being made. Finding the balance of accommodations and strategies that push our children toward independence and success is a process of trial and error. We're unlikely to hit the bullseye the first time we shoot. But, if we're all in the room working together on brainstorming and willing to try new things, we're on our way to accomplishing our goals.

Co-parenting between Households

When I talk to neurodivergent kids who go between households due to custody or other arrangements, I'm always impressed by their awareness of what is acceptable in one environment but not in another. The self-regulation necessary to transition frequently between different households with different expectations is sig-nificant. Add into this the fact that many of our 2e kids struggle with transitions and inconsistencies, and you'll understand how important it is for co-parents to work to build consistency between environments as much as possible.

Proactive planning that involves your child's input is one of the best ways to attempt to establish this consistency between environments. What works and what doesn't for homework routines, household expectations, or leisure activities? How can this be established and clarified so everyone is on the same page to eliminate power struggles or manipulation ("Well, at *Mom's* house …")? Depending on your relationship with your co-parent, communication about these expectations may be dif-ficult. If you have a trusted professional who knows and works with your child – a teacher, school counselor, or mental health professional – asking them to help facilitate a conversation about how to consistently support your child's needs in varied envir-onments might create a neutral zone to develop strategies that can be carried out in multiple environments.

Arranging for additional therapies or tutoring around a custody schedule can also be a difficult task. Depending on the level of collaboration and conciliatory communication between co-parents, I've seen kids whose parents each want them to see their own counselor or who will allow a child to receive dyslexia tutoring, but only on the weekends they are with the other parent. Some professionals are hesitant to work with families with shared custody arrangements. When you are seeking help for your child, one of the questions to ask is how they communicate with parents in shared custody arrangements. Do they consistently communicate and share information with both parents and not only the parent who has attended an appointment with the child? Bringing a parent into the conversation and making sure they don't feel like decisions are being made without them is one of the most effective ways a professional can establish a healthy, collaborative relationship with a child's parents.

Chapter Reflection

♦ Within your relationship with your co-parent, what was the process of finding a diagnosis like? Did you reach the same awareness and comfort with the diagnosis around the same time or did one take longer than the other? How did that influence your relationship with each other and your relationships with your child?

♦ Does your child go between various environments with different individuals in parenting roles and different expectations in each? Is there a way to communicate with those in parenting roles to establish consistency between environments?

♦ Are there any situations where you and your co-parent could work on proactively communicating and establishing a parenting plan to maintain consistency for your child? How would a shift in this area influence the interpersonal dynamics in your home?

Note

1. Greene, Ross. "ALSUP 2020 Collaborative & Proactive Solutions." Lives in the Balance, 2020. https://livesinthebalance.org/wp-content/uploads/2021/06/ALSUP-2020-1.pdf

PART

III

The Five Skills All Twice-Exceptional Kids Need

The chapters in Part III of this book are dedicated to the skills that twice-exceptional people need to be successful in a world that wasn't always created for them. There is a balance within these chapters of skills that will help neurodivergent kids and teens to advocate for the environmental changes that help them to be the most successful, as well as skills that parents can help them develop so they are better able to navigate and respond to their world.

Each twice-exceptional child is different. Not every 2e kid needs help with impulse control and not every 2e kid needs to work on developing social relationships. Feel free to skip around to the chapters that seem like they would benefit your child the most. Each chapter includes specifics about why a twice-exceptional child might struggle in the area and ideas for how to develop the skills in your child.

Our ultimate goal is to create children who are resilient, independent, and successful. Each of these tools is necessary to achieve those goals. Addressing them from a neurodiversity-affirming perspective means we are honoring our children's personalities and preferences while helping them to develop the skills that will allow them to navigate the world with confidence.

DOI: 10.4324/9781003237532-10

7

Skill #1 – Self-Advocacy

When planning this book and deciding on what order to put the chapters, I originally had self-advocacy as the final chapter of this section. For some reason, it sometimes feels that self-advocacy is the thing that comes after a child really understands themselves and their needs. Some of the other skills seem more important. Self-advocacy is a nuanced skill, dependent on emotional regulation, communication skills, and perspective taking. Ultimately, though, I want to make sure that self-advocacy isn't an afterthought. No matter what your child's difficulties, finding appropriate ways to self-advocate is the foundation for all of the skills that we are hoping to build. Without self-advocacy, we fall into the trap of having kids feel like the world is happening "to" them; we need them to be actively involved every step of the way.

Almost all types of neurodivergence are going to be a part of an individual's make-up throughout their lifespan. Finding ways to build appropriate self-advocacy skills empowers our children to create the structures and supports around them that they need and carry this skill through their lifetime. When we teach appropriate self-advocacy, kids learn that their way of learning, thinking, and doing is allowed, even if it isn't what everyone else is doing. We teach them to problem solve and find flexible solutions to their situations, giving permission to get un-stuck in whatever way works best for them.

DOI: 10.4324/9781003237532-11

This permission to look for new solutions is life-changing. I've worked with clients who never considered the fact that they could ask to use voice-to-text as a pre-writing activity. Or that they could video their presentation instead of standing in front of an entire class, petrified with social anxiety. I've worked with neurodivergent adults who were afraid to ask for accommodations at their workplace because they had never been offered before, as a child or in adulthood. For our twice-exceptional children, who do an excellent job at masking their difficulties, the internalized message based on never having been offered accommodations because they "seem okay" can last a lifetime. There is no reason for any of us to white-knuckle it through life. Teachers and employers are learning the importance of flexibility and offering accommodations to all; self-advocacy by a neurodiverse community helps to make the world a more supportive place for everyone.

We talk a lot in education about "scaffolding." Scaffolding is a construct that developed from educational psychologist Lev Vygotsky's theory of the zone of proximal development (ZPD). ZPD focuses on the fact that a child is most able to grow and learn when they are challenged to reach just beyond their current level of ability. Scaffolding is the term used to describe the supports we give children to help them move from one level to the next. Imagine a piece of scaffolding at a construction site. It can be constructed higher or lower, depending on where the construction is taking place. The supports, ladders, and barriers can be easily moved to allow workers to scale tall structures safely and compete the work that needs to be done. In the educational setting, we talk about scaffolding for learning. We want to provide the right amount of support for kids – not too much, not too little – that brings kids to their zone of proximal development. In the zone of proximal development, kids are pushed *just to the edge* of where their learning is taking place. It asks them to stretch just a little bit further than they're already able to do. Just how building muscle requires us to gradually lift heavier weights, learning requires us to gradually do more difficult tasks. Scaffolding is the structure that makes sure we don't stretch too far and burn out or give up.

Scaffolding relates to self-advocacy because we want our kids to eventually be able to construct their own scaffolding around themselves. What supports do they know they need to reach that next level? What tools will provide those accommodations and support? Is it something they can implement on their own and just need to self-advocate to ask permission to use them? Or do they need to self-advocate for assistance from those around them for the scaffolding to be effective?

There will be times that we see our kids struggling and recognize that they need that next level of scaffolding erected to help them reach their goal. It is easy for us to say, "Woah! Hang on! Let me help you with that!" When we come to the rescue, though, we remove our kids' autonomy and sometimes we need to watch from a distance and wait for our kids to ask for our help. Jessica Lahey's book *The Gift of Failure* explores the need for our kids to experience distress and how we do a disservice to our kids when we do too much for them. Stepping back and providing opportunities for both self-advocacy and failure is a necessary step toward growth for our 2e kids.

Some kids may feel extremely comfortable asking for help, but when they don't get "enough" help, they get frustrated and shut down. Learned helplessness occurs when children develop a habit of refusing to take risks without extensive support and assistance from others. The learned helplessness is not related to an inability to do the task, but an aversion to the risk or work involved in it. Appropriate self-advocacy is helpful for students who experience learned helplessness because it can teach them how to identify their needs and request accommodations in a way that provides an appropriate amount of support while allowing them to continue to stretch to the next level on the top of that scaffold.

Self-advocacy skills are not only necessary in the academic environment, but at home and in social relationships, too. 2e kids who struggle with both self-regulating their emotions and self-advocacy are prone to developing poor boundaries within social relationships, either becoming too rigid and uncompromising or allowing people to walk all over them.

When Is Self-Advocacy Needed?

Twice-exceptional kids need self-advocacy skills because their needs can go unnoticed so easily. Depending on their personality and type of neurodivergence, they are also the kids who often struggle the most to develop these skills. Self-advocacy is useful in many environments and relationships: the academic setting, with peers, or with parents.

Kids often need to self-advocate at home. They may find themselves in situations where self-advocacy with a sibling would be beneficial; there are also many occasions where self-advocacy is a helpful strategy with parents. Your kids may feel extremely comfortable making their needs known in your household, but perhaps they could use some strategies to communicate more effectively. Appropriate self-advocacy from children at home can reduce power struggles, improve parent–child relationships, and build the skills necessary for self-advocacy in other environments outside the home. Additionally, children who go between households due to custody arrangements, yet thrive on consistency, often find themselves needing to speak up about their needs.

Chapter 5 explored how you can foster healthy communication with your child. How you respond to their efforts to self-advocate greatly influences how they choose to self-advocate (or not) in situations outside of the home. When we can hear their requests without getting defensive and model a healthy conversation with our children, we build their confidence in advocating in other environments and situations. Whether it is asking for a later bedtime, more video game time, or a change in the routine for chores, taking the time to hear their request (without giving a knee-jerk "no" response) and talking through it with them is a great opportunity for building this skill, while building our relationship with them at the same time.

At school, twice-exceptional kids benefit from self-advocacy related to both their abilities and their difficulties. Deb Douglas wrote *Self-Advocacy for Gifted Learners*. It provides a framework for gifted kids to advocate for their education by seeking opportunities for challenging curriculum and other education needs. On episode 8 of *The Neurodiversity Podcast*, she shared about her first experience helping kids learn to self-advocate and the response she got that pushed her forward to find ways to continue teach kids to self-advocate.

> We weren't asking [gifted kids] what it was they needed. It was kind of top-down. We were telling them what they needed and sometimes that worked really well, and sometimes it didn't work at all. … My first experience asking kids what they need, and I really just got blank stares and shrugs because the kids didn't know what they needed necessarily. They didn't know how to articulate it. They didn't know they had a right to something different.[1]

Advocating for accommodations and other support is also necessary in the academic setting. I've worked with too many twice-exceptional clients to count whose teachers (usually middle and high school students) had absolutely *no clue* that the student was entitled to accommodations through a Section 504 Plan or IEP. Because these students are often in upper-level classes and because they are often masking their difficulties, it doesn't occur to the teachers to consider that they might need support, and, unfortunately, some schools are better than others at communicating those needs to teachers to ensure plans are followed. A lot of 2e students are afraid to ask for help or remind their teachers that they are entitled to accommodations because they believe the teachers know they are supposed to provide them, but don't want to do so. They frequently are also uncertain about how to address the issue. It can be embarrassing when you are one of only a few twice-exceptional students in an advanced or honors-level class to ask to take a test in a separate setting or ask for a copy of the day's lecture notes.

Utilizing self-advocacy within peer relationships can be one of the most complex and difficult areas. Friendships and peer interactions are tricky to navigate for the most social children; our twice-exceptional kids can find themselves traversing a minefield based on their own level of social savviness. Whether attempting to negotiate a truce with a friend over a minor disagreement or handling the stressful situations resulting from bullying behaviors, self-advocacy with peers is frequently difficult. Additionally, this is an area where our kids really have to handle the situation on their own; there isn't a ton we can do to follow up with a child's peer group the same way we can with a school professional.

Developing Self-Advocacy Skills

There is an evolution that occurs as children learn how to appropriately verbalize their needs in a way that is both effective at achieving their intended goal and is received as it is intended. We can identify where our children are within these stages, what is causing some discomfort related to self-advocacy, and develop skills that will help them become more self-sufficient in having their needs met in a variety of situations.

Stage 1: Recognizing When Help Is Needed

In order to begin the process of self-advocating, kids must first have awareness that there is something amiss. Because twice-exceptional children have such a unique composition of strengths and struggles, they may have difficulty recognizing that they are having trouble. Unchallenging academic settings can lead to internalized beliefs that, because they are smart, they shouldn't need help. When things become unmanageable, they get stuck. (This is one reason why appropriately challenging curriculum for high-achieving students is so necessary.)

Helping kids learn the signs that show they need assistance is one strategy to build self-advocacy skills. We can help them to recognize the types of thoughts, emotions, and actions that indicate they might need help. If you notice a situation where self-advocacy would be helpful, facilitate a conversation with your child to explore these three factors; or, if the situation has already occurred, debrief about what happened and ask your child to reflect on what happened.

- ◆ *Thoughts*: Identifying unhelpful self-talk is a key piece of recognizing when help is needed to improve self-advocacy skills. It is helpful to describe self-talk to kids and teens as the thought bubbles above a cartoon's head, describing the words they are thinking. For kids who struggle with verbalizing their thoughts, it can be helpful to create a short storyboard or comic strip using thought bubbles to help facilitate this awareness. Some of the thoughts someone might have who needs to engage in self-advocacy could be "I can't do this," "I should just quit," or "This is too hard." Brainstorming a list of thoughts your child has had when they needed help is a good conversation starter and reference to go back to when discussing self-advocacy in the future.

◆ *Emotions*: Knowing what feelings are a cue that it might be time to self-advocate is important to help children be proactive in seeking help. Finding the "just right" emotion word and developing an awareness of the physiological signs (body signals) of those feelings is a step to acting before getting overwhelmed. Is your child feeling: Helpless? Confused? Frustrated? How does their body signal those emotions? Through sweaty palms, an upset stomach, or a clenched jaw? Chapter 8 on emotional regulation explores the importance of emotional literacy and how to build the ability to identify and describe emotions.

◆ *Actions*: Talk with your child and look for clues in their behavior that indicate that they need help. Some kids might appear distracted or start engaging in preferred (but perhaps discouraged) activities, like reading in class or playing with their phone. Others might notice they begin chewing on their pencil or pacing around the classroom. When twice-exceptional kids build awareness of what those behaviors look like, they can serve as an indicator to assess whether self-advocacy would be useful.

Creating Comics to Build Awareness of Emotions

Many of the skills discussed in this book rely on the cognitive-behavioral-based skills of recognizing thoughts, emotions, and actions. Depending on a child's age and their specific strengths and struggles, articulating these through conversation can be tricky. Using the format of a comic strip can help to differentiate between these three components. Thought bubbles clarify self-talk, actions are represented by what the character is doing in the comic, and emotions can be indicated with body language and facial expressions.

One reason I really like this activity and use it frequently is that it helps to differentiate between thoughts and feelings; for example, when I ask a client how they were feeling in a situation, I often get replies like "I felt like I wanted to hit him" or "I felt like I wanted to leave school and never come back." I work with the kids to help understand that these aren't really feelings, but thoughts. If you remove the "I felt like" at the beginning of each sentence, you're left with a thought: "I wanted to hit him," or "I wanted to leave school and never come back." Drawing thought bubbles over comic strips is a helpful way to make the difference more concrete.

Stage 2: Finding Help

Once kids realize that they can't manage a situation on their own, they need to know where to go for help. In many situations, the person to ask for help might appear obvious – your teacher in the classroom, your parents at home, or your friend if it is a social situation. However, there are other factors that may inhibit a twice-exceptional child from either realizing who is the best person to ask or feeling comfortable asking that person for help. Planning in advance for what obstacles might prevent self-advocacy helps kids to feel comfortable initiating that plan when it is needed.

Another integral component of finding help is the feeling of safety in certain environments that a twice-exceptional child may not have. Vulnerability is required anytime someone needs assistance from another person. Asking for help can feel like a weakness, and twice-exceptional children who've flown under the radar by compensating for their struggles with their intelligence may have a difficult time finding someone they trust enough to request help from.

If your child is in this stage of developing self-advocacy skills, have a conversation with them about how they feel about finding help. See if you can find any obstacles that had gone unnoticed when seeking support in the past. You can use the following questions as a starting point for your conversation.

♦ *What beliefs prevent you from asking for help?* It is always interesting to hear the theories that twice-exceptional kids have developed about asking for help. Some of those theories have moved from theory to law in the 2e child's brain. The one example that always stands out to me (and that I've heard over and over) is that they truly believe that they aren't allowed to ask for help. This is especially true related to academic difficulties. The rationalization is that it is school, and they are supposed to learn and do the work on their own; if they don't, it is cheating or unfair to the other students. Perfectionism prevents them from believing asking for help is acceptable. Another common situation is the belief that asking for help causes them to burden the person providing the help. Some kids just want to "do it on [their] own." Often, the act of providing explicit and individual permission to the child by the person offering the help can alleviate some of these fears.

♦ *What do you believe will happen if you ask someone to help you?* Some twice-exceptional children and teens might believe that asking someone to help them will cause that person to think negatively about them. They might worry about feeling embarrassed in front of their peers or the adult who is asking for help. They may be concerned that the person is simply going to dismiss their concern or request and tell them to "figure it out on their own." Helping your child articulate what exactly they believe will happen when they ask for help will identify any barriers that can be removed.

- *In what situations do you think people can help you? Are there situations where you think nobody can help you?* It is difficult to find help if you don't believe anyone can help solve your problem. If there are situations your child can identify as unsolvable (at least by other people), try to coach them through finding alternative ways that someone could help in a situation. For example, a child may be correct in thinking that their teacher can't solve a problem related to a peer situation, however, the teacher might be able to help them look at the problem from a different perspective that relieves some of the stress it is causing. Emphasizing the benefit of just having an outlet to talk through the problem aloud can often provide insight the child didn't realize they had within them.

- *Who are the people that you trust who can help you?* Brainstorm a list of trusted adults and peers who can help solve problems. It may even help your child to list the specific types of problems each person can help solve.

- *What do you expect from someone who tries to help you?* Setting realistic expectations about what a person who is trying to help can and cannot do is helpful for many neurodivergent kids. Kids and teens who've developed learned helplessness may want more help than is appropriate. Others who are just getting familiarized with asking for help benefit from knowing what types of responses they are likely to receive after asking for help.

While we want our children to attempt to recognize and solve their own problems, it is understandable that a child may not feel comfortable with discussing a concern directly with a person in an authority position. Self-advocacy can include seeking an ally and requesting help from them. A child talking to the teacher in their gifted education or special education classroom and asking for help communicating with their classroom teacher can be effective self-advocacy. Coming home and talking to a parent and asking for intervention is also a method of self-advocacy. It is appropriate for us to intervene in some instances; while we want to encourage our children to handle situations on their own with our support and coaching behind the scenes, sometimes we may need to be the liaison to make sure their voices are heard.

One final consideration related to helping kids through this stage of self-advocacy: Past trauma can play a role as it relates to your child finding help. Children and teens who've experienced trauma may require extended time to develop relationships where they are comfortable enough to trust a person and take the risk of asking for help, and a trusting relationship is the keystone of asking for and receiving help. Additionally, while perhaps not rising to the level of trauma, the long-term impact of being a twice-exceptional learner in a school setting that doesn't recognize or serve their needs can also cause long-term damage to faith in the ability of teachers or other school personnel to recognize, validate, or support their needs.

Stage 3: Communicating Needs

Kids who are aware that they need help and know where to find it are ready to initiate the task of effective and appropriate self-advocating. Twice-exceptional learners benefit from direct and explicit conversations about how to accomplish these types of tasks. These types of social skills are one area where the asynchrony of twice-exceptional kids hits hardest because those around the twice-exceptional child assume that something as "simple" as asking for help should be no problem for a child who can expound on the nature of the space-time continuum. However, it is often best to take nothing for granted and work with your child to develop a specific plan or strategy to self-advocate.

Planning the logistics of asking for help is often useful so kids feel prepared for making their request. Is this an impromptu request in class or at home that can be made verbally? Is it easier to advocate through an email or note? Should the request be made at a specific time and place (like between classes) or is watching for a pause in a conversation or natural break in the action appropriate? There is comfort in planning and knowing what to expect when making a request. If your child worries a lot about things not going according to plan, they may feel more comfortable using email or another method of communication that doesn't require face-to-face interaction. While developing confidence to make requests independently and in person is a good goal, meet your child where they are. Writing their own email with a request is a step closer to independence than having a parent facilitate the conversation with a teacher or talk to another parent about a peer situation. Encourage any attempts to advocate on their own.

Helping twice-exceptional kids express their requests in the most effective way also empowers them to feel more confident when self-advocating. If a child has been attempting to self-advocate but is receiving negative feedback, tweaking the way they make their requests might help. As their parent, you probably are already aware if the way they frame their requests is working against them. Teaching twice-exceptional kids to make effective requests is a skill they will use throughout their lifetime.

When I help kids develop self-advocacy skills, we talk a lot about how to frame requests. We frequently script out planned phraseology for self-advocacy or use role play to practice these steps in advance.

- ◆ *Be specific.* When kids clarify exactly what they need, the helper is going to have a better idea of how to help. Someone who states "I need help understanding how to show my work when I'm isolating the variable in this equation," is going to find an easier solution (and more positive response) than someone who says, "I don't know what I'm supposed to do." Whether the situation is based on an assignment or a general life situation, being exact about the problem is a good way to start a request.
- ◆ *Use neutral language.* Self-advocacy shouldn't come across as complaining or griping. Also, while some twice-exceptional kids may not understand or value the importance of being cautious with how we state our opinions, helping them engage in perspective taking on how another person may react to their request is beneficial. If we need someone to help us, we don't want to hurt their feelings. "The way you decided to rearrange all the seats in the class is not helping me pay attention at all!" can be rephrased as "I'm having difficulty focusing at my

new seat." Diplomacy goes a long way in getting what we want and need.

◆ *Offer a suggestion or possible solution.* When kids self-advocate with a possible solution in mind, they are showing that they are attempting to solve the problem on their own before asking for help. This lets the helper know that they aren't just giving up. This might also be a description of solutions already attempted. For example, a student might let a teacher know they already re-read the instructions and asked a classmate for help, but they still need help.

◆ *Ask for their help or permission.* A simple "Can you help me?" wraps up the final component of the self-advocacy script. If a possible solution was offered earlier, requesting permission or other ideas is a good way for kids to frame their request: "Do you think that would be okay, or do you have any other ideas?"

Sample Scripts

Here are a few sample scripts. It may be helpful to share these with your child while you are working on building self-advocacy skills.

◆ *Social anxiety*: "I get really nervous when I'm called on during class and I'm not expecting it, but if I'm called on when I raise my hand or I know I'm about to be called on, it helps me get ready. It would really help me if we could come up with a signal, so I know you're going to call on me. Do you think that might work or do you have a better idea?"

◆ *Unchallenged in class*: "I love math! I like it so much that I am already pretty comfortable doing the work that we're covering because I taught myself through online videos over the summer, but now I'm having trouble paying attention because I already know what we're learning. I was wondering if there might be a way for me to do a pre-test to show that I know how to do this and then I could work on some harder math. Could we try to work something out?"

◆ *Distractions at home*: "I know it is important for me to get my homework done and turned in on time, but my sister keeps interrupting me while I'm trying to focus. I was thinking that there might be a place around the house where I could do my homework without so many distractions. Can you help me find a place that would be better?"

◆ *Negotiating activities with peer*: "I want to play with you at recess, but I know you like to play other games that I don't always want to do. Maybe we can figure out a way to take turns so that we both get to do a little of what we want and still get to spend time together. Do you want to try that?"

Chapter Reflections

◆ What are your child's strengths and difficulties related to self-advocacy? Do they avoid confrontation at all costs, are their attempts to advocate perceived as abrasive, or do they fall somewhere in between?

◆ How does your child self-advocate at home? How do you respond to their attempts to self-advocate? Is there a way to improve healthy self-advocacy in your home?

◆ What are your boundaries for where you feel stepping in to advocate for your child is too much? What signs do you look for that indicate that your child's self-advocacy efforts aren't being received and it is time for you to intervene?

Note

1. Douglas, D. (2018, May 2). A guide to self-advocacy [Audio blog interview]. Retrieved from https://neurodiversitypodcast.com/home/2018/5/2/episode-8-a-guide-to-self-advocacy

8

Skill #2 – Emotional Regulation

Learning to manage our emotions is a skill that takes a lifetime to learn, and one that I've never known a single person to have mastered. However, being tuned into our emotions is vital for our success – at school, at work, and in our relationships. We need to understand the significance of the problem and react at a commensurate level; we don't want to overreact *or* underreact.

Neurodivergent kids may have difficulty regulating their emotions for many reasons. Emotional dysregulation is a frequent component of some neurodivergent diagnoses. ADHDers and autistic people frequently struggle with regulating their emotions. The main impact of mood and anxiety diagnoses is the impact on one's ability to regulate emotions. Gifted kids have heightened awareness and the ability to logically comprehend complex ethical and moral topics, but don't have the life experience and emotional regulation skills to manage the discomfort that can come along with them. Neurodivergent twice-exceptional kids are living in a world that wasn't created for them, triggering all kinds of difficulty with regulating emotions.

Normalizing emotions is a key part of learning to regulate them. One of the fundamental components of regulating emotions is removing judgment of those emotions. Reframing emotions as comfortable and uncomfortable – instead of good and bad – is one step to helping kids step back from their emotions. Emotions

DOI: 10.4324/9781003237532-12

serve a purpose, and we need to help neurodivergent kids understand that purpose. Emotions are the communication from our brain to help us guide our decision-making and assessment of a situation. If we can look at emotions objectively, instead of believing emotions like angry or sad are emotions that should be avoided at all costs, we can choose how to act on them, instead of allowing our emotions to drive us.

Emotional dysregulation in neurodivergent kids can look very different from child to child. While all kids experience emotional dysregulation in varying levels as they grow, there are a few characteristics of dysregulation that are found more frequently in neurodivergent populations.

Built-In Anxiety

Whether neurobiological in origin or caused by environmental stressors, many neurodivergent kids experience anxiety that is built into their daily lives. The effort required to mask their areas of weakness takes a toll and can make them feel like they are constantly on edge. Many characteristics directly associated with a neurodivergent diagnosis are triggers for anxiety. For example, autistic people frequently struggle with unexpected changes; using cognitive flexibility to manage those situations isn't easy for many twice-exceptional kids and they are put into situations requiring them to do so on an almost-daily basis. Gifted kids with learning disabilities are going to experience a sense of anxiety surrounding academic tasks that are difficult for them.

The fear of not fitting in or being seen as different can be a major stress for 2e kids. Twice-exceptional kids who have difficulty with social relationships are often constantly on edge. They worry about whether something they've said or done has been misinterpreted; they stress out, trying to figure out if what was just said to them should be interpreted literally or if there is an alternate meaning they didn't catch. Trying to catch and interpret hidden social rules is both anxiety-provoking and exhausting, leading to a reduced capacity to regulate emotions.

Twice-exceptional kids who struggle with executive functioning skills feel anxious about trying to avoid getting in trouble for not paying attention or not having their work completed. Often placed in upper-level classes, the requirement for staying organized and on top of work can be overwhelming, leading to high levels of stress.

When a twice-exceptional child's difficulties are directly related to a discrepancy in their ability compared to their achievement in an academic area, the pressure of keeping up with schoolwork is intense. The awareness a child has when they can't get the words from their mind to the paper or can no longer compensate with their background knowledge when reading material gets longer and more difficult is extremely distressing.

Each of these situations leads to an underlying level of anxiety for twice-exceptional kids that may be relieved occasionally, but rarely is completely gone. This level of nonstop anxiety means a child's level of tolerance for handing stressful situations is limited, and their bandwidth for regulating their emotions is constrained.

Perfectionism and Stress

The advanced cognitive skills of twice-exceptional kids make them prime candidates for developing signs of perfectionism. Although research doesn't consistently show that gifted individuals exhibit characteristics of perfectionism more frequently than the general population, there are environmental influences that may foster distress when accomplishments don't reach expectations for bright kids. For example, young gifted children often learn without much effort at all. Unless provided with an appropriately challenging curriculum, there isn't much we can do to prevent them from internalizing the message that they are smart. They begin to expect academic work to be easy; at some point, when things become difficult, they may struggle with this blow to their ego. They may ask themselves, "If being smart is equivalent to learning fast and school being easy, what does it mean about me when school gets hard?"

Twice-exceptional learners who have difficulty with flexible thinking are also prone to intense frustration and stress when assignments or work are imperfect. They may have experienced a similar progression as described above and don't know how to handle work that gets difficult. I've also worked with clients who believe that because the teacher is asking them to do something, that they "should" be able to do it with complete accuracy. One perfectionistic client prone to catastrophic thinking would go from a fear of missing one or two questions on a test to believing he was destined to be jobless and destitute as an adult in a single sentence.

With or without perfectionistic overtones, stress for twice-exceptional students plays a role in whether they can regulate their emotions. "Spoon theory" is an analogy developed by the disability community and adopted by the neurodivergent community to describe the finite number of stressors one can handle each day. Each stressor we encounter requires us to use a spoon and once it is used, it is gone for the day. The number of spoons can vary day to day, and we don't always know in advance how many spoons we will have available to us in a day. However, once we are out of spoons, we are out. For twice-exceptional kids, running out of spoons can mean there are no spoons left to regulate emotions. Helping kids recognize how much tolerance (aka "spoons") they have and self-advocate when their stress level is about to spill over is necessary for them to effectively regulate their emotions.

Alexithymia

Some neurodivergent people have a difficult time recognizing and describing their emotions. This difficulty is described in psychology as "alexithymia." There are multiple factors that can influence one's ability to identify internal emotions. Some people experiencing depression exhibit temporary characteristics of alexithymia; they describe feeling numb or flat when depressed. Autism can be connected with alexithymia, which is one reason autistic people may have difficulties labeling and sharing their emotions. Alexithymia is not exclusive to either of these diagnoses, and neurodivergent kids with other diagnoses may also show signs of alexithymia.

Alexithymia can cause difficulty with regulating emotions for several reasons. One of my autistic clients described their experience with alexithymia as knowing that something wasn't right, but not knowing exactly what it was. The inability to pinpoint the cause for feeling distressed or uncomfortable was an additional stressor. It is difficult to find a way to regulate emotions if there is uncertainty about what the emotion is, let alone what might be causing the feelings.

Often, we think about emotional dysregulation as "too much" emotion, but people with alexithymia often struggle from the converse. Emotional dysregulation that involves overreacting brings images of the child who is melting down over a small situation or blowing up over a perceived injustice. Underreacting, sometimes caused by alexithymia, can also be problematic. Sometimes a little stress over grades is okay because it motivates someone to do something about it. When there is trouble in a social relationship, one person may get frustrated if they perceive that the other person isn't reacting strongly enough. Other times, people with alexithymia may struggle with not noticing their emotions gradually increasing until they are so distressing, they are past the point of no return.

Some people with alexithymia can attribute some of the difficulties to sensory processing differences. Chapter 3 discusses the impact of sensory differences in neurodivergent people. There is more to our sensory profiles than the common five senses described. Our proprioceptive and vestibular senses help us with awareness of how our body is interacting with the outside world; our interoceptive sense is necessary for noticing sensations within our bodies, sending those messages to the brain, and interpreting what they mean. If suddenly you notice your stomach is hurting, can you identify the reason it is hurting? Are you hungry? Nervous? Sick? Need to go to the bathroom? We are reliant on the sensations our bodies experience to help us notice and clarify our emotional state. If the interoceptive sensory system is doesn't interpret those internal messages correctly, it becomes much more difficult to know how we are feeling.

Rejection Sensitivity

Research and understanding about rejection sensitivity in neurodivergent populations are growing. Frequently cited as a concern for ADHDers, rejection sensitivity manifests as a hypersensitivity to perceived criticisms. "Rejection sensitivity dysphoria" is the term used for the subclinical characteristics experienced by ADHDers.

Even without an ADHD diagnosis, twice-exceptional people are at risk for experiencing increased levels of rejection sensitivity. Developing an increased response to perceived negative feedback can be the result of how much (or how little) support neurodivergent kids experience in certain environments. It only takes a few highly emotional events to sear those fears in one's memory and cause someone to be on the lookout for an incoming rebuke.

The difficulty with rejection sensitivity is that the heightened emotional response to experiencing the feelings of being pushed away is often swift and out-of-proportion to the alleged injustice. The response might be one of anger, with the intent to retaliate. It might be an inability to forgive, even after an apology has been offered. The fear of rejection is persistent among relationships and might make others feel as though they are walking on eggshells to avoid a possible offense.

The I-CAN Method for Regulating Emotions

Establishing a goal to develop emotional regulation skills with your child is one of the best skills you can teach them. Michelle Borba wrote the book called *Thrivers*, and one of the basic tenets of this book is that kids who are resilient and thrive in our world aren't necessarily born into the world with the skills needed for success. She was the guest on episode 79 of *The Neurodiversity Podcast* and shared her advice on resilience for parents.

> We've got to dispel this myth on resilience that it's all locked and we can't do a thing about it. Our children, we are raising them in a very uncertain world, who knows what's going to come down the pike later on, unless we turn this around and help our kids. ... And our goal right now is to raise up a generation of strong kids in mind and heart. And this is doable.[1]

Because our emotional development is constantly changing as we mature and have different levels of awareness, the I-CAN method is useful for kids and teens of all ages. The conversations and skills discussed in the steps naturally evolve based on your child's development. The signals that lead to emotional dysregulation in a seven-year-old are much different than those facing a fifteen-year-old, and their ability to identify and recognize those causes is much different, too. As your child gets older, point out the growth that you see. Emphasizing your own growth over time also helps to normalize the experiences of choosing different ways to react to situations and emotions.

The steps necessary for developing emotional regulation skills can be broken down into four steps. This four-step process is called the I-CAN method. Its acronym is useful not only for you to remember the steps, but you can use the terminology and framework as you work with your child to develop emotional regulation skills.

The four steps of the I-CAN method are:

1. *Investigate*: Step one involves investigating and building awareness surrounding dysregulation. Recognizing and understanding the signals that indicate when emotions intensify are the necessary foundational skills before initiating strategies to regulate their emotions.
2. *Communicate*: Step two asks kids to find ways to communicate about feeling dysregulated. Building emotional literacy skills is a key component to being able to communicate when dysregulation is occurring.
3. *Activate*: In step three, kids activate problem-solving skills by assessing the size of the problem and responding appropriately through using cognitive flexibility to understand their dysregulation.
4. *Navigate*: Step four involves navigating the emotional dysregulation with specific strategies that can be used to return to a regulated state.

Explicit teaching and building these skills during times of regulation is a necessity; don't wait until a crisis arises to attempt using the I-CAN method. I often tell the families in my office that building emotional regulation skills is just like training for a marathon. You train and build your muscles gradually through practice and slow growth. You might begin with running one mile, and then two, and slowly work on getting faster and running farther. When race day arrives, you are prepared. If attempts to use these skills are only made when a crisis (aka "race day") arrives, you won't be prepared and will be frustrated that you aren't able to use the skills as well as you'd like. This is also a helpful analogy to put into context any "failures" after an attempt. Just because you didn't win your first race doesn't mean you quit; it just means you train more!

Step One: Investigate

Step one of the I-CAN method asks kids to investigate the causes of emotional dysregulation and the signals that dysregulation is on the horizon, and become familiar with patterns of behavior when they are feeling emotionally dysregulated. Developing this awareness is a key component to being able to proactively initiate strategies to regulate emotions before they become too intense to manage. By the end of this book, you'll notice how frequently I bring up helping our kids develop a level of self-awareness. This self-awareness is necessary if our goal is to help our kids reflect on their behaviors and emotions and use that reflection to modify how they are interacting in the world.

Use the following topics to guide the conversations you have with your child to investigate their emotional regulation patterns. These questions are open-ended and might lead to more questioning. Encourage your twice-exceptional child to create their own hypotheses and seek out additional information. Build hypothetical situations, some realistic and others far-fetched, to engage in thought experiments and stretch their beliefs and understandings. Harness the critical thinking skills of your gifted child's brain to build a greater awareness of how emotions influence their lives.

◆ *What is the purpose and nature of emotions? Why do we experience emotions?* Help kids recognize the nature of emotions to make them less powerful. Understanding that emotions are based on chemical reactions to our brains and hormones that humans have developed to help us stay alive builds understanding of what is happening physiologically when our emotions grow.

◆ *Is it better to make decisions based on emotions or logic?* Emotions are a way our bodies communicate with us about a situation, but they are only a piece of the puzzle; like detectives, we have to gather other evidence before having a full picture of any situation. Using only logic to handle a situation doesn't validate the very real experience of how we feel. Dialectical behavior therapy discusses how to blend the emotional mind and the logical mind to create the wise mind when handling emotional situations.

◆ *What is a "gut reaction" or "gut feeling"? When is acting on a gut feeling helpful or hurtful?* We want kids to notice those immediate, visceral reactions and learn to pause before acting. This isn't always easy for many of our impulsive neurodivergent kids! Validating that the emotions exist and drawing attention to them is a step toward being able to make different choices on how to act. It also provides the opportunity to ask ourselves why we react the way we do.

◆ *How long do emotions last? Are emotions temporary? Why does it feel in the moment like the emotion will never subside?* One of my favorite analogies related to emotions is to think of them as though they are waves. If you stand at edge of the ocean, you can watch waves approach the shore. Sometimes you can see them at a distance and sometimes they arrive without much notice. They might approach slowly and gently wash over your toes, or they might have unexpected force that can cause you to have to regain your balance. But the one thing that all emotions have in common is that they are temporary; the waves always return to sea. Remembering that emotions are temporary reminds us that even when we are distressed, we aren't stuck in those emotions forever.

◆ *What do you notice about how your body feels when you are getting dysregulated? How do different emotions feel in your body?* Learning to identify and take cues from the physical symptoms that indicate dysregulation is a big step toward developing strategies to regulate uncomfortable emotions. For younger children, instead of talking about the emotions, create a diagram of their body and label the different body signals they receive for various emotions.

◆ *Are emotions always "right" or is it possible that emotions are "wrong" at times?* One of my favorite therapeutic quips is, "Feelings aren't facts." (Another take on this: "Just because you think it, doesn't mean it is true.") Helping kids realize that *how* you are feeling doesn't always consider all pieces of situation can remove some of the power of intense emotions.

◆ *How do emotions mix? What emotions are more visible and which emotions stay hidden? Why is it easier to show some emotions and not others?* Secondary emotions are often the ones that the outside world sees. Often, anger is a secondary emotion. When we look a little deeper, the underlying emotion might be embarrassment or fear. It is often easier to show an emotion like anger because it is outward facing and directed toward another person or situation. Acknowledging underlying emotions often takes a level of vulnerability that many of us aren't comfortable showing.

Along with the ongoing conversations you have with your child about emotions, it can be really useful to investigate the patterns that your child experiences leading up to and following emotional dysregulation. Collecting data in this way provides a chance for kids to reflect on their own experiences. Keeping it a judgment free zone (there aren't any rewards or consequences associated with this tracking) helps kids to feel comfortable monitoring this information. It is common for kids to feel uncertain about tracking this because of negative feedback or experiences they've had in the past based on their difficulties regulating emotions.

There are many methods to do this. One way to track emotional regulation patterns is to create a daily chart or calendar to notate patterns of dysregulation. Identify a specific measure you'd like to monitor. For example, your child may choose to track how stressed they felt each day on a scale of 1–10. Or they rate their day with colors based on how well they felt they managed their uncomfortable emotions. Be specific about what you are measuring and select a specific time that you'd like to touch base about their reflections. Kids who are more comfortable with or enjoy technology might find an app they can use to track their mood or create a spreadsheet. Whatever method you choose, use the information as a conversation starter to investigate what factors influence your child's dysregulation.

If you feel that your child needs a little more support or structure to this activity, one resource I have found helpful is Michelle Garcia Winner's "Zones of Regulation" books. These popular books are used by counselors, special educators, and occupational therapists throughout the country. Emotions are categorized into four sections based on the level of activation you experience when feeling them. The Blue Zone represents feeling low or down; the Green Zone is when you're feeling focused, calm, and ready to learn; the Yellow Zone signifies feeling just a little dysregulated, like being excited or annoyed; and, when someone is completely out of control and feeling rage or bouncing-off-the-walls silly, they fall in the Red Zone. The curriculum is useful for creating a shared language between environments and focusing on finding regulating strategies for the body for any type of dysregulated emotions.

Step Two: Communicate

The C of the I-CAN method for emotional regulation stands for "communicate." Once your child has investigated the purpose of emotions and how to identify them, we need to help them learn to communicate with others about what those emotions are. Communicating emotions is necessary for emotional regulation for several reasons. In order to self-advocate when emotionally dysregulated, being able to communicate how you are feeling is important. Additionally, having the power to put feelings into words gives a sense of control over what may feel like unmanageable emotions.

There are a range of reasons why communicating emotions may be difficult for twice-exceptional children. Some kids may struggle with identifying their emotions due to alexithymia. Others may fear sharing their emotions because they worry they aren't *supposed* to feel certain ways or be wary of past experiences where their emotions were invalidated. Students dealing with perfectionism may have internalized the culture of "toxic positivity" – the belief that one must always be positive and optimistic, to the detriment of honoring and sharing uncomfortable emotions. It can also be uncomfortable to give others a glimpse into our inner world of emotions. Or, children may feel they don't know the "just right" word for an emotion; it may be hard for them to identify a nuanced emotion with the vocabulary that is accessible to them.

Many twice-exceptional children also have a strong affective memory. A past experience that holds an exceptionally strong memory might resurface when they are faced with a similar situation or emotion. For example, processing through uncomfortable emotions with one of my neurodivergent clients often leads us through a string of memories and emotions back to the time they were bullied in elementary school. They would rather avoid talking about uncomfortable emotions at all because they know that those strong emotions are going to resurface.

One of my favorite strategies to teach clients when we are working on emotional regulation is "Name It to Tame It." I was originally introduced to this strategy through the book *The Whole Brain Child* by Daniel Siegel and Tina Payne Bryson. By labeling an emotion with the "just right" emotion word, we create a brief window of time to reflect on exactly what we are feeling, which can then help us understand why we are reacting in a certain way. This strategy aligns with mindfulness skills of separating oneself from emotions by stepping back and recognizing the emotion in order to remove some of its power. If we can help kids learn to pause and assess their emotions, it can help them get a bit of distance from the emotion and choose their actions more consciously. Elaborating on the analogy that emotions are like waves, taking a moment to examine an emotion and name it is like catching the wave and surfing on it; it is still there, but you are in control of how you interact with the wave, instead of the other way around.

To build the skill of communicating emotions, we need to help our children build emotional literacy. Reading literacy involves the combined skills of fluency (being able to quickly identify letters and phonological sounds) and comprehension (understanding what the combination of words means). Emotional literacy requires the same skills of fluency and comprehension. Being emotionally literate requires rapidly identifying emotions and understanding what they mean about a situation. We can scaffold the skills of emotional literacy for our children through explicit coaching and gradually building on those skills.

◆ *Model labeling your own emotions.* Taking the time to articulate your emotions aloud shows kids how emotions vary and normalizes the experience of having a range of emotions throughout each day. Think of this as narrating some of your thoughts and adding on the emotion word; don't worry about conversing about the emotions with them. This is really an opportunity for your child to learn simply through watching you. You might say, "I'm feeling so exhausted from this long day and I am unmotivated to finish up the laundry," or "I'm feeling a little uncertain about a work project, but I'm also excited to figure it out." Try to find specific emotion words, when you can, and identify mixed emotions about situations when possible.

◆ *Label your child's emotions for them.* Using a reflection of emotion, label your child's emotions for them, if they can't find the words. Interpret their actions and words and check with them to see if you are close. For example, "It looks like you are feeling excluded from your friends. Is that pretty close to how you're feeling?" or "I can tell you are feeling proud of how you did during your swim meet because of your smile and how excited your voice is while talking about it. Would you agree that you feel proud?"

◆ *Normalize talking about both comfortable and uncomfortable emotions, without judgment.* Kids may have internalized feeling that talking about positive emotions is bragging or sharing negative emotions is complaining. Help kids understand the difference and set up a culture in your home where it is okay to talk about all feelings.

◆ *Provide or create tools for children to use as prompts to find the "just right" emotion word.* Before kids are able to access an emotion word from their own mind, they might need to work from a menu of choices. There are many ways to do this. Doing an internet search for "vocabulary of emotions" or "emotion wheel" can provide a variety of options you can print and keep accessible. (I have a laminated emotion wheel that is handy at all times during sessions.) The Mood Meter app is another great tool that can be downloaded and kept close at hand on a phone or tablet. You can also use your kids' verbal ability to help them create their own tool to find the "just right" emotion word (see the activity in the text box "A Range of Emotions").

A Range of Emotions

To help build your child's awareness of the varying intensities of emotions and how emotions can be mixed, you can create a tool to help them recognize the ranges of emotions. This activity is probably best for primary elementary kids up through about sixth grade, although you know your child and how they learn best. You'll need paper (cardstock is best), colored pencils or crayons, scissors, and paperclips. You may also need index cards or sticky notes, and a thesaurus or access to the internet.

1. Talk to your child about what they believe are the foundational emotions. These are the emotions that when the intensity of them is varied, you experience

different emotions. Think of the characters from the Disney/Pixar movie *Inside Out*. When I do this activity with clients, we usually end up with anywhere from four to six emotions; usually, they are a variation of happy, angry, sad, scared, surprised, or disgusted.

2. Draw one thermometer to represent each foundational emotion. Choose a color for each feeling and color in the thermometer; shade the thermometers lighter at the bottom and darker toward the top to indicate the intensity of the emotions.

3. Brainstorm a list of emotion words that aligns with each foundational emotion. For example, the "happy" list might include excited, enthusiastic, pleased, content, etc. Write these words on a list or individually on sticky notes or index cards.

4. Rank each category of emotion from *least* intense to *most* intense. If you've chosen to write the emotion words on index cards, it can be helpful to physically move and rearrange the cards. If you've written the words on a list, they can be ranked by writing a number next to the words.

5. Write the emotion words along the side of the thermometers, with the least intense emotions at the bottom of the thermometer and the more intense emotions near the top.

6. Use scissors to cut a straight line up the middle of the thermometers. Slide a paperclip on each thermometer to use as a moveable indicator of how intense the emotion is.

7. When discussing emotions with your child, ask them to move the paperclips on each thermometer to indicate their feelings on each scale. In addition to providing the emotional vocabulary your child needs to describe their emotions, it recognizes that varied and sometimes conflicting emotions can both exist simultaneously.

Beyond building emotional literacy, the act of communicating through verbal communication may be difficult for your child. Some neurodivergent people get so overwhelmed by emotions they cannot speak while they are dysregulated. Working with your child to find alternative ways for them to communicate with you is helpful. This might involve communicating non-verbally or choosing a time and place to communicate after the dysregulation has subsided. I've seen families use a variety of strategies; the ultimate goal is to encourage communication at whatever your child's ability level and gradually improve their communication.

If your child becomes nonverbal when they are dysregulated, one way to help them communicate is to establish a system for your child to use hand signals to express their level of dysregulation. Perhaps indicating with fingers their level of dysregulation on a scale of one to five or a system of thumbs up, in the middle, or down can provide an alternative way for them to communicate how they are feeling. Writing notes may help your child to communicate. Keep a small notebook or dry erase board handy and ask your child to write how they are feeling or what they need; you may also communicate with them in writing, asking questions ("Would you like to be alone or for me to stay with you right now?") that require only a basic response. If your child is unable to provide a signal or write, verbalizing what nonverbal signals that you are watching for also gives a way for your child to respond when they are ready ("Your face is covered now because you're upset; I'll know you are ready for me to help you when you can uncover your face.").

Twice-exceptional kids have a wide range of communication abilities. Taking their cues and meeting them where they are is a neurodiversity-affirming strategy to gradually move them toward independently being able to communicate their emotions.

Step Three: Activate

In step three of the I-CAN method for emotional regulation, we ask kids to activate their problem-solving skills to manage uncomfortable emotions. This step requires using logic and cognitive flexibility to assess a problem and find ways to look at the problem from a variety of angles. This step moves kids toward recognizing their ability to reframe their thoughts and emotions that surround a problem and not feeling that they are unable to escape the influence of uncomfortable emotions.

Many neurodivergent kids struggle with cognitive flexibility. Part of this can be due to executive functioning difficulties; being able to think flexibly about situations is an executive functioning skill. Some twice-exceptional children have a hard time with cognitive flexibility because they tend to be very black-and-white with their thinking overall. Perhaps this is related to their neurodivergent diagnosis; rigid thinking patterns are characteristic of autism. It may also be a characteristic of their personality or a culmination of past experiences. Kids who often feel out of control may cling to rigid thinking patterns because it is consistent and feels safe. Learned helplessness may also drive kids to reject opportunities to think about situations flexibly. "I've never been able to manage this before," they may think, "so why would shifting my thoughts help now?"

Whatever the reason for difficulty with cognitive flexibility related to emotions, it is a necessary ingredient for the I-CAN method for emotional regulation. In order to activate the systems that can help reduce feelings of overwhelm, anger, or disappointment, kids need to be able to look at problems from different angles.

Cognitive-behavioral therapy often involves looking at problems and putting them in proportion to the actual situation. This is the "don't cry over spilled milk" step of emotional regulation. A proportional response to a triggering event requires someone to look at it within the greater connect of the situation. You can help your child understand how to look at a problem in proportion to the big picture through ongoing conversations and cue words to help them realize the actual size of the problem. One of my go-to analogies to help kids conceptualize what happens when they make a problem bigger than necessary is a brief "experiment." I give them a quarter and ask them to hold it between their thumb and forefinger. I then ask them to bring it near their face and hold it close to one eye, while closing the other eye. I ask them to describe what they can see. The coin will take up most of their field of vision and they won't be able to see much else, other than the coin. Then, I ask them to hold the coin at arm's length and describe what they can now see. The coin is much smaller, and they can see the rest of the room. We bring the analogy back to the problem and discuss how when we hyper-focus on a problem and examine it closely without giving it space, it is easy to feel that the problem is huge and insurmountable. When we take a step back, we can see the problem within the larger context of our daily lives and realize that we don't need to get "stuck" on a single way of viewing the problem or one way to try to fix it.

Another great activity to help kids activate their problem-solving skills to work through emotional regulation is one I learned from Lisa Van Gemert. This strategy is most effective when working to overcome a worry about something that may happen in the future. Lisa wrote the book *Perfectionism: A Practical Guide to Managing Never Good Enough* and described the possibilities model to overcome a fear of failure on *The Neurodiversity Podcast*:

> [To use the possibilities model] You would say, "What's the best possible thing that could happen here?" Then, "What's the worst possible thing that could happen?" And then, "What is most likely?" First of all, if the worst possible case happens, you've already had that emotional discussion with yourself so it's not as devastating. Number two, is that you start to see a pattern, "Oh, I frequently see the worst case scenario as the most likely scenario and that's just not accurate."[2]

Using this strategy to put problems into proportion with their likely outcomes can help to move kids away from paralysis or anxiety about what may happen. Sometimes when I do this activity with clients, we get a little silly with it, to help exaggerate the influence of black-and-white thinking.

Ronnell is in middle school. He is anxious about an upcoming math test. He received an 85 on the last test and is stressed because depending on how this next test goes, he may have a B on his report card (which has never happened before).

Worst case: "If I do poorly on this test, I'll probably get a B on my report card. Then I won't be able to get into the honors math courses in high school, I won't get a scholarship to college, I'll have to work through college and end up dropping out and eventually I'll end up homeless."

Best case: "This will be the easiest test ever, I'll get an A+, and my teacher will not make me take any tests the rest of the year because I'm such an awesome student."

Most likely: "I'll do fine on my test. I probably will still get an A on my report card, but even if I don't, it is only a quarter grade and won't make much difference in the big picture."

Maya is in elementary school. She is afraid to confront a friend, Emmie, who is jealous and has been unkind to another friend, Taryn. Maya wants to maintain a friendship with each, but feels caught in the middle.

Worst case: "I try to talk to Emmie, but she gets really angry and starts a fight with me. Then she gets everyone in the class to hate me, too, and then I don't have any friends. Then Emmie decides to be best friends with Taryn, and I don't even get to be her friend, either."

Best case: "When I talk to Emmie about Taryn, Emmie immediately realizes that she was being mean and apologizes to me and Taryn. We all become best friends and never argue with each other ever again."

Most likely: "Emmie is kind of upset when I talk to her about how I feel about how she is treating my other friend, Taryn, but she says she will try to be nicer to her. She agrees to try to talk to me when she feels left out or jealous instead of being mean to Taryn."

Tamir is a high school student and is stuck in a class that he doesn't like. The teacher doesn't provide accommodations for Tamir's disability and won't listen when Tamir tries to advocate for himself. Tamir is afraid he's going to "blow up" at the teacher in class, but is also afraid to ask his counselor to switch to a different class because he might have this teacher again in the future.

Worst case: "I get really panicked in class because I can't get my work done in time and I lose my temper and start crying in the middle of class. The teacher points it out in front of everyone and asks why I'm acting this way and then I lose my temper, yell at the teacher, and storm out of the class. I get suspended for being disrespectful and am forced to stay in the class because my counselor thinks I'm being dramatic."

Best case: "When I ask the teacher for extended time on the test, he apologizes profusely and announces he's going to retire that day because he can't believe he made such a mistake."

Most likely: "I can go talk to my counselor or my parents and explain the situation so they can help me advocate, since the teacher won't listen to me. The teacher will make the accommodations and won't make me feel guilty about it."

TABLE 8.1 Worst case/best case/most likely scenarios

Each of the strategies that is tied to activating the problem-solving skills necessary for emotional regulation ties the problem, whatever it might be, to something concrete. Our emotions are generally very abstract and nebulous, which can make managing them seem difficult. One method that offers another way to activate the problem-solving circuit of emotional regulation is one my twice-exceptional clients love because it leverages their logic by moving the conceptualization of emotions to the tangible realm of quantities: specifically, money.

Emotional price-tagging is an activity you can do with your child to help them assign values to various types of problems and reactions. This uses the concept of ratios to establish what is a "penny problem." A penny problem is small in value and not worth overspending. Like most of the interventions I use with twice-exceptional students, I often let kids take the lead as we work through the steps of this activity, so use the steps and model as a starting point, but feel free to be creative with your child or teen as you create a system that works for you.

The intention of this activity is to help evaluate the "worth" of certain types of problems or reactions to help put them in proportion to the problem. Building a stronger awareness of when our emotions are out-of-whack with the thing that caused them allows us to take action to find alternative solutions to our problems. Another benefit to this activity is the development of a common language that can help to communicate with your child about the level of their reaction. Instead of telling them they are overreacting, we can ask them to self-evaluate how much "money" they are spending on a problem. We can ask them if something is a "penny problem" and if they are "spending or saving" their emotional energy.

Step three of the I-CAN method for emotional regulation asks kids to find ways to think flexibly about situations that cause uncomfortable emotions, put their emotional reactions into proportion with the size of the problem, and activate their problem-solving skills by realizing the situation is something that is manageable. They're now ready to move onto the final stage of emotional regulation: navigating through the discomfort and dysregulation.

How to Use Emotional Price-Tagging

Emotional price-tagging is an activity to complete in advance of emotional dysregulation to build awareness of disproportionate emotional responses. Once you and your child have developed the language and system of emotional price-tagging, you can use the strategies as a tool to activate problem-solving skills when emotions become dysregulated. You'll need paper and something to write with to complete this activity. Your child may also enjoy using construction paper, index cards, or markers to make actual "price tags," but this is optional.

1. Begin by talking about the value of money and why it is important to only spend the "right amount" on certain purchases. Discuss how we don't want to overspend because we'll waste money. Tell your child that you are going to work together to create a list of prices (some kids also like to call it a menu) to different types of problems and the value of the type of emotional response each deserves.
2. Brainstorm a list of possible problems that would elicit an emotional response. Come up with about 8–10 possible problems.
3. Create a second list of possible emotional reactions. This might include no reaction at all, to an eye roll, to a full meltdown. Try to come up with about 6–10 different levels of reactions. List these in order from smallest to biggest reaction.
4. Assign each emotional reaction on the list a monetary value. Start with the lowest value as a penny for the smallest emotional reaction and move up from there. You and your child can determine the increments of value, but this works best if they are generally both at somewhat regular intervals and within the range of what is not an exorbitant amount

of money. For example, your list might include penny, nickel, dime, quarter, dollar, five dollars, ten dollars, and twenty dollars.

5. Use the valued emotional reactions to establish a monetary cost to each of the possible problems listed in step two. How many of these could be penny problems? How much is your child typically "spending" on their reaction? Are they spending frugally or are they wasting their emotional energy (aka money) on their out-of-proportion reactions?

After completing this activity, refer back to the values of emotional reactions when you are processing dysregulation with your child. An extension to this activity could involve using it as a framework to self-evaluate how situations were handled afterwards. You could make a chart to include a brief description of the situation, the expected value of the situation (how much was it "worth"?), and the amount of emotional money your child "spent" on their reaction. Did they overspend or spend appropriately? Did they find a "sale price" and even react at a lower value than what the normal cost is? Track how much money they spend or save throughout a week.

Step Four: Navigate

So far through the I-CAN method, we've helped our neurodivergent kids investigate and understand the signals that lead to their emotional dysregulation, find ways to communicate with others when they are feeling dysregulated, and activate problem-solving strategies and build cognitive flexibility to empower them to act to reduce emotional dysregulation. The final step of the I-CAN method to build emotional regulation asks kids to take this information, integrate it into their understanding of their emotional reactions, and navigate the dysregulation. How are they going to get through the emotional dysregulation? The specific strategies in this section are built to help twice-exceptional kids choose the strategies that work for them to persevere and bounce back from emotional setbacks.

Many of my clients often feel that something is wrong with them if they aren't happy all the time. I'm not sure if this is an effect of the constant highlight reel of other people's lives they see on social media or if they've somehow built up the perception that others are always feeling happy. Either way, I work with my clients to help them know that while dysregulation isn't a healthy baseline, feeling "mostly content, most of the time" is generally a fairly good goal for managing our mood. The frustration that kids feel when they think they are "failing at life" because they aren't happy all the time is damaging. In order to navigate uncomfortable emotions, we need know what our target is and sometimes our target is to get through the discomfort.

Navigating emotional dysregulation can be broken down into three segments. First, we ask our kids to *reset* through mindful awareness of dysregulation. Then, they can *reframe* the thoughts that are influencing the discomfort. The final step of navigating their emotions is to *rebound* after the dysregulation to a state of calm.

Reset

Once again, leveraging the cognitive ability of our twice-exceptional children is a useful tool to help them learn to reset. While the terms mindfulness and meditation might cause some of our concrete thinkers to recoil, helping them understand the science behind them can help them become more willing to attempt to use them. We can teach our students about the fight/flight/freeze response and how our bodies sometimes sense danger when there is none. This sends our brains into survival mode, increasing our heart rate, breathing, and thought patterns. Using deliberate breathing techniques and other mindfulness strategies helps us get our brains out of survival mode.

I like to explain mindfulness as a way to consciously choose what we are going use to fill our minds. Instead of the rapid-fire thinking and crashing emotions of being intensely emotional and feeling out of control, we are going to choose where to direct our focus. This may mean imagining some visual in our mind, talking to ourselves so we can "hear" our self-talk, or intention-ally pointing our attention to the physical sensations we are experiencing. Some kids (and adults!) may feel frustrated when they find their minds wandering; learning to identify when that wandering mind occurs and gently recalibrating our attention is a slow process. The most important key to doing this is not to become so frustrated that giving up feels like the best option.

One of the most important components I instill in my clients as we work to develop their skills to reset their dysregulation is that learning how to de-escalate emotional overwhelm is a skill that must be built slowly. Practice makes progress (never per-fect!) and we can't improve a skill without working on it in times of calm in order to be able to access the skill in times of stress. Whichever strategy they choose to try is up to them, but finding a time and place to practice it to build the "muscle memory" needed for times of intense dysregulation is key. There are a few strategies that I've found my neurodivergent clients prefer:

◆ *Counting breaths*: Sometimes clients don't like breathing exercises that require them to breathe in or out for a cer-tain count of breaths, or to hold their breath. They may feel that it makes them more stressed or feeling breathless. The counting breaths technique is nice because it doesn't require someone to do anything different with their breathing. I describe it to my clients like this: "Just take a moment and focus on your breathing. You don't have to change anything about it. Just notice your breaths in and out and start counting: As you breathe in, think to yourself *one*, then as you breathe out, count in your head *two*, then with your next inhale *three*, then out again *four*. Keep counting your breaths until you get to ten and then start back over at one. Keep counting your breaths and focusing on the counting until you feel calmer." I also suggest they attempt to slow and deepen their breathing, if they find their breathing is rapid and shallow.

◆ *Straw breathing*: I keep a handful of coffee stirrers in my office to teach my clients how to do straw breathing. Coffee stirrers work best because they are narrow and restrict the flow of air and require us to breathe slowly as we exhale. To begin this exercise with your child or teen, start with a coffee stirrer or straw. Say, "First, let's take a minute to note how our bodies are feeling. How do our muscles feel in our shoulders, our jaw, our legs, our stomach? What emotions do we notice? We're going to take a deep breath into our lungs and then try to push it out through the straw and we want it to make it last as long as possible. Ready? Go." Once everyone has released all of their breath through the straw, talk about what physical and emotional changes are noticeable. Remind your child that we aren't looking for total peace, just to feel a bit closer to calm. This strategy can also be utilized in any environment without the coffee stirrer or straw.

♦ *Under pressure*: Deep pressure is often regulating for kids with any type of sensory issue. How many of you have already purchased weighted blankets for your kids (or yourself)? For this mindfulness activity, instead of focusing on the sensations of breathing, we're going to teach our kids to use their own bodies to apply deep pressure to calm themselves. A modification of other progressive muscle relaxation techniques, this strategy is nice because it can be used in multiple environments – in the car, the classroom, or at home. Kids do need to be able to be seated while they are using this technique. While they are sitting, guide them through the activity. "We're going to start by placing our feet flat on the floor and our hands flat on the tops of our legs. We're going to use our hands to apply pressure to the tops of our legs while using your feet to push our legs up against our hands. Pay attention to all of the things you notice in your body while we do this. Ready? Okay, go. Let's hold it: one, two, three, four, five, six, seven, eight, nine, ten. Now take your hands and put your palms facing upward underneath your thighs and we're going do the opposite. Pull your arms and hands upward, like you are trying to pick yourself up while pushing your feet as hard as you can toward the ground. Let's hold it: one, two, three, four, five, six, seven, eight, nine, ten. Okay, now let's relax and shake out our muscles." Bring the conversation back to the focus on the shifts your child feels in their body and emotions.

◆ *Pulse pattern*: For this activity, we're going to ask our children to find their pulse and count their heartbeats. It is generally easier to teach them to find their carotid pulse in their neck, but if they are able to find it in their wrist, that is fine, too. For younger children, you may help them find their pulse on their wrist and use a washable marker to show them where to place their fingers to find their pulse. Once they find their pulse, guide them though this exercise. "Now, we're going to count our heartbeats. We'll count in our heads while we focus on the patterns of our pulse. How fast or slow does it go? Does the speed stay the same or change? Does it feel stronger or weaker at different points? Let's count one hundred beats. Ready? Go." Mindfully attending to our pulse helps to move our minds away from any dysregulating thoughts or emotions going through our minds. Talk about what patterns they noticed. If you practice this when they are both calm and more elevated, help them notice the differences based on their emotional state.

Reframe

Being able to notice uncomfortable thoughts and reframe them in a way that makes them feel manageable is a huge skill for navigating emotional dysregulation. This cognitive flexibility gives us the opportunity to redefine our experiences in a way that feels manageable and moves us away from helplessness. Twice-exceptional kids may have trouble with reframing their thoughts because of their different brain wiring; they may also have been so repeatedly exposed to the negative thought patterns that escaping them feels impossible. Creating new thought patterns can be tricky.

When I'm working with kids to help them understand the benefits of neuroplasticity and how they can retrain their brain to process situations in new and different ways, I use the analogy of traveling through a wooded area. If someone is going for an extended camping trip in an area where nobody has lived before, they might set up camp and need to find a way to reach fresh water. Once they've found the best way to get from their camp-site to the stream and have traveled it, the underbrush and weeds will gradually give way to a beaten down path. The more that path is traveled, the easier it will be to use. Neural pathways in our brains are the same. If we have a certain sequence of neurons that fire to bring us from one thought to another, the more we travel that pathway, the more automatic it becomes. If we want to forge a new neural pathway – a new way to react to a situation – we have to do the hard work of beating down the brush and weeds to gradually create the path. It takes a conscious and concerted effort to build a new pathway, but it can be done.

Reframing thoughts is different than using positive thinking. I am grateful for the shift away from always feeling like we need to think positively, because it isn't always realistic or helpful to put a silver lining around situations or neglect the very real implications of a difficult situation. The phrase "toxic positivity" has been coined recently to highlight the pressure to sweep uncomfortable thoughts, emotions, and experiences under the rug, leading to internalized misery and neglected trau-matic experiences. Our bright kids won't fall for fake positivity, and when we try to present it as an option, they'll call us out for shifting a situation so far from reality that it is unlikely to happen or negating the very real uncomfortable emotions that are associated with the situation. Reframing thoughts is a way to put our thoughts into perspective and focus on finding a solu-tion. Reframed thoughts are manageable.

Exaggerated negativity is the counterbalance to fake posi-tivity. Exaggerated negativity occurs when we take negative thoughts and bring them so far around that we act like they are insignificant or don't matter. A kid who feels they don't have any friends may attempt to insist they don't want any friends and that having to worry about having friends is dumb. This exaggerated negativity is another defense mechanism to deflect uncomfortable emotions and distance oneself from the work that may be required to resolve a situation.

Pointing out black-and-white thinking and finding ways to reframe it with your child is a great conversation. Once your child has learned the skill, during conversations, it is easy to prompt them with a quick "Is there a better way we can reframe this situation?" When explaining this concept to your child, helping them recognize the difference between fake positivity and reframed thoughts can help to highlight that the point isn't to pretend the problem doesn't exist, only that it is something they are strong enough to handle.

Reframed thoughts also rely on dialectical thinking. Dialectical thinking is a strategy frequently used in dialectical behavior therapy. It involves recognizing that two statements that appear to be opposite on the surface are not mutually exclusive. They can both be true at the same time, moving from an "either/or" mindset to a "both/and" view. For example, "I'm feeling isolated at school *and* there are people who I can build connections with," or "I'm doing my best *and* I can work to try to do better," takes two statements and ties them together, recognizing that even though something that is uncomfortable is true, it isn't the *only* thing that is true, and there might be other possible factors or solutions to handle a situation.

One note of caution about reframing thoughts with neurodivergent kids. We have to be really careful that we don't fall into the trap of denying or ignoring the lived experiences they have had. Behavioral techniques in general should be used with caution for neurodivergent kids because they are often framed from a standpoint of neurotypicality. For example, telling a neurodivergent child to reframe their thoughts about how someone is treating them can mean they ignore bullying when they should set healthy boundaries. In these situations, offering reframes that are empowering to action, such as "I can choose who to spend my time around," or "I can ask for clarification if I don't understand what they meant," can be more helpful. Awareness of thoughts continues to be a helpful tool, and choosing the thoughts to focus on helps us gain emotional regulation, but we want to make sure we aren't causing a situation where our neurodivergent child is being gaslit into not believing their own experiences.

Your child says ...	Fake positivity / exaggerated negativity	Reframed thoughts
"I don't have any friends."	"Lots of people like me." "Nobody likes me, but that's fine because having to worry about friends is really just a waste of time and a pain."	"I have some people who are friendly to me. I think I can try to strengthen those friendships, even if it might take time to get there."
"I'm going to fail all my classes."	"I know it is the last week of the quarter, but that's plenty of time to bring my grades up to all A's." "I'm never going to college anyway and grades don't matter, so I'm just not even going to bother trying."	"My grades are in a tough spot this semester, but I think I can make a realistic plan to improve them."
"I hate my life."	"My life is really great, and I don't have any reason to feel sad."	"Life is hard right now and I can find ways to get through it. I've gotten through difficult times before and I know this feeling is temporary."
"I'll never pass this test."	"I'm sure if I just try really hard, I can get a good grade on this test." "The teacher has made these tests basically impossible to pass. It doesn't even matter if I study or not."	"Even though I've had trouble in this class before, I think I can come up with a plan to try to improve my test grades." "This test is going to be hard, but I'll try my best. Even if I don't do well, my other grades in the class will help my average."
"I hate school. Nobody there cares about me."	"School can actually be a really fun place and if I get to know more people, I'll find out there are lots of people who care about me." "There is no way anyone at school is ever going to notice or care about me."	"I'm having a hard time at school right now. I think if I ask for help, there are some people who care enough to try to help me."

TABLE 8.2 Reframing thoughts

Rebound

When used in the moment of emotional dysregulation, the steps involved in the navigate step of the I-CAN method happen rapidly. Take a moment to *reset*, another few minutes to *reframe*, and finally, reenter a regulated state to *rebound*. When we are working with our children to help them rebound from dysregulation, we want to debrief with them and provide an opportunity to self-advocate.

Eventually, our kids will be able to walk themselves through this process, where they can ask themselves the questions necessary to work through what has happened and establish the next best steps. But, while we are scaffolding the support they need, we have the opportunity to influence that inner voice for the long term.

One of the most difficult things about the rebound phase of regulating emotions as a parent is finding the "just right" time to help them debrief. Is it best to jump on the debriefing immediately? Should you wait until the next day? What is the magic Goldilocks zone – not too early, but not too late – for debriefing? There is definitely some trial and error involved in developing these strategies, but you likely already have an idea of your child's natural rhythm following an episode of emotional dysregulation. The goal is to talk about it at the point where it is fresh enough to remember so the discomfort is still close enough to motivate change, but with enough distance that the conversation won't launch your child back into emotional dysregulation. A few times, when a family has arrived for an appointment and an incident that needs to be processed is in the immediate past, I find myself explaining why it is a "good thing" that the event happened. It isn't good that the event occurred, but it is good that I have the chance during a session with my client to process the incident while it is still fresh. This is the time where the change occurs.

Consider your own emotions, too, when you are trying to find the best time to debrief and help your child rebound. If your emotions are still heightened or you suspect you might find yourself launching into a lecture, try to give a little more time before talking to your child. Our goal during this phase is to help our children learn the skill of rebounding from dysregulation, and that involves their active participation in the process. If they find themselves listening to a drawn-out explanation about what they did wrong or what they should have done instead, not only are we taking away from them the opportunity to learn and develop their own resources, we are also allowing them to tune out, and they'll probably forget everything we say anyway.

When you are ready to talk to your child about their emotional dysregulation, here are some ideas to guide your conversation. Part of this process is walking through the steps of the I-CAN method to reflect on how each step was (or wasn't) integrated.

- ◆ Tell me about what happened from your point of view. (Investigate)
- ◆ Was there anything that led up to the situation? (Investigate)
- ◆ How could you identify that you were beginning to get upset? Encourage them to consider physical signs of discomfort and emotional/cognitive signals. (Investigate)
- ◆ What emotions did you have throughout the situation? (Communicate)
- ◆ Did your emotions change throughout the situation? How? (Communicate)
- ◆ Do you feel like your reaction was too little, too big, or about the right size for the situation? If you've introduced emotional price tagging, this would be a place to integrate that terminology. (Activate)
- ◆ Where are the points that you feel like the situation could have taken a different path? Try to direct their focus to cognitive flexibility for their own controllable actions, not those that were caused by another person. (Activate)
- ◆ When you started to notice you were getting upset, what actions did you take? Did you try to reset your system? (Navigate)
- ◆ What thoughts were you having during the situation? Did you try to reframe them? Are there some we can try to reframe now? (Navigate)

◆ What should we do to help prevent this in the future? Is there anyone who can help put those systems in place? (Navigate)

Taking the time create a plan for future situations is one of the most empowering tools we can provide to our children. Jot down some ideas that come out of this conversation. Modeling this method of developing a new plan after the old plan hasn't been effective is a tool we want our kids to be able to implement independently as they get older. Problems and discomfort are the catalysts for change. Developing a plan gives both a sense of control and a sense of relief. Let's help our kids rebound from the discomfort and grow.

Using I-CAN to Reduce Emotional Dysregulation

Cori is feeling dysregulated because she misunderstood the directions on an assignment, and when she asked for clarification, her teacher made a joke that Cori hadn't been paying attention. Cori recognizes the signs of dysregulation (*Investigate*) as her heart starts to beat fast, she feels her face get hot, and tears are stinging her eyes. She mentally labels the emotions she is experiencing; she is feeling embarrassed and is still confused, which is triggering the secondary emotion of anger (*Communicate*). She remembers that she wants her reaction to match the size of the problem and tries to think of a solution (*Activate*). She takes a moment to think about how she will handle this situation (*Navigate*) and focuses her attention on doing a brief reset of her body through a mindful breathing exercise. She pays attention to her thoughts and challenges the faulty thinking with a more realistic reframe: "I'm not stupid, I just made a mistake. This is a little thing that nobody will remember." After she is feeling calmer, she approaches her teacher, asks for clarification on the assignment, and self-advocates by explaining to the teacher how the public joke made her feel.

Chapter Reflection

- ◆ How does your child handle emotional regulation? Are there situations where they are better able to manage their emotions than others? Can you identify why some situations might be easier than others for them?
- ◆ How well does your child identify their emotions? Are they comfortable disclosing that information to a few trusted people?
- ◆ When your child begins to become dysregulated, do they notice in advance or are they already completely dysregulated by the time they notice?
- ◆ Does your child have any coping skills that help them navigate emotional dysregulation? Is there a way to amplify or support those skills while also building new skills?

Notes

1. Borba, M. (2021, March 11). Moving beyond surviving to thriving [Audio blog interview]. Retrieved from https://neurodiversitypodcast.com/home/2021/3/11/episode-79-moving-beyond-surviving-to-thriving
2. Van Gemert, L. (2018, April 4). Overcoming perfectionism [Audio blog interview]. Retrieved from https://neurodiversitypodcast.com/home/2018/4/4/episode-6-overcoming-perfectionism

9

Skill #3 – Executive Functioning

Almost all of the diagnoses associated with twice-exceptional learners include some level of struggle with executive functioning. Executive functioning skills are based in the prefrontal cortex of the brain. Because brain development begins with the brain stem and gradually moves up and forward, the prefrontal cortex is the last area of the brain to develop and come online and is often responsible for some of the asynchrony that can be seen in some gifted learners. Being twice-exceptional exacerbates that asynchrony.

Executive functioning skills are responsible for keeping things running smoothly in our brains. Like the office manager who makes the decisions about who gets in to see the boss and when, answers the phones, manages the budgets, organizes and orders supplies, and coordinates the schedules of the employees, the job of the prefrontal cortex is to expedite and clarify our actions and help us make decisions that take all factors into account. When one executive functioning skill is offline, it can throw the entire system out of whack.

Executive functioning skills include both decision-making skills and behavioral regulation skills. The decision-making skills include planning/prioritizing, organization, time management, working memory, and metacognition. Behavioral regulation skills include response inhibition (impulse control), emotional

DOI: 10.4324/9781003237532-13

regulation, sustained attention, shifting focus, task initiation, cognitive flexibility, and task persistence. These are the skills that are necessary for many of the day-to-day tasks. Basic tasks, like completing homework, for example, require several executive functioning skills to each act in tandem with each other. Table 9.1 shows how tasks require multiple executive functioning skills.

Can Executive Functioning Skills Be Taught?

If executive functioning difficulties are neurologically based, can they be improved? Can we teach kids how to have better task persistence, or are kids who have a difficult time with organization, time management, or planning destined to struggle throughout their entire lives? Can executive functioning skills be improved?

The short answer is "yes," but for our twice-exceptional kids, we need to consider some factors that influence their ability to improve executive functioning skills and, also, reevaluate what we specifically mean by improving their executive functioning skills. The concept of neuroplasticity indicates that we can rebuild and shift the way our brains function with intentional structure and support. But even more important for neurodivergent kids is to learn new and different ways to mitigate and accommodate our struggles. An approach that integrates these two avenues – structured and intentional guidance on building executive functioning skills plus support to find accommodations to reduce the impact of executive functioning difficulties – is one that will help your child build the skills necessary for success with executive functioning difficulties.

Because twice-exceptional learners compensate with their areas of strength, it may not be until they are older that their executive dysfunction becomes apparent. A child who struggles with sustained attention during class may be able to glide through their early school years only paying attention to a small percentage of the instruction that takes place; as content becomes more difficult, the inability to maintain their focus has more of an impact and causes more distress than when they were younger. The expectations for young people to manage certain tasks

Decision-making skills

	Task: completing homework	Task: cleaning the bedroom	Task: finishing a long-term school project
Planning/prioritizing: identifying the various steps necessary for completing the task and recognizing which tasks are most important and need to be completed first	Thinking ahead to remember what materials to bring home from school	Assessing the various tasks that need to be done and creating a plan for what order to do them in	Identifying each of the steps necessary to complete the project and developing a strategy to get each finished before the due date
Organization: systematically maintaining materials in a way that allows for knowing where an item is and finding it with ease	Knowing where to find the assignment (like having it written in a planner) and being able to find the physical materials for it	Categorizing and sorting the various items and having a systemized place to put each	Managing materials necessary for the project and keeping them in a designated and organized space
Time management: accurately estimating how long a task will take and mentally arranging tasks to ensure enough time is available to complete the tasks as desired	Understanding how much time is available after school and estimating how long the homework will take	Estimating how long various portions of the task will take without over- or underestimating each task; starting the task with enough time to make the progress desired/expected	Assessing each step of the process and determining how long each step will require; beginning each task in a timely manner so there isn't a time crunch near the deadline
Working memory: short-term memory; hearing or seeing something and retaining and reusing the information mentally	Retaining the directions for the assignment in short-term memory and accessing them as necessary while working on the assignment	Recalling all of the specific steps or suggestions from parents about what needs to be completed to clean room	Quickly reviewing prior work completed on the project and remembering and implementing information on current step

Metacognition: investigating a current thought process or skill and determining if modifying the strategy or skill is beneficial; "thinking about thinking"	Reflecting on the assignment as it is completed and evaluating whether it is being completed correctly or not	Evaluating the process for cleaning and whether there is a different strategy that might make the process more efficient	Reviewing and shifting plans and methods for projects if the current approach isn't working
Behavioral regulation skills			
Response inhibition: stopping an impulsive behavior; thinking before one acts	Rushing through an assignment to get it done quickly without paying attention to detail and missing important steps or instructions	Resisting urge to play with toys found while cleaning or start a new (more interesting) activity	Making intentional choices while completing the steps of the project; preventing impulsive decisions or work that have to be revised in the future
Emotional self-regulation: monitoring one's emotional state and making adjustments for the situation as necessary	Managing frustration if homework is challenging	Handling feelings of disappointment when cleaning results in missing out on preferred activities; persisting on task through feelings of discomfort	Tolerating boredom when the long-term project is no longer new and exciting
Sustained attention: focusing on a single task for a continuous amount of time without getting distracted or pulled off-track	Keeping attention on a task for the sustained amount of time necessary for completing the homework	Continuing to make progress on identified task of cleaning without stopping and restarting	Using time that is allocated for working on the project effectively; working in short bursts with few distractions
Shifting focus: regulating attention appropriately and moving between activities without emotional dysregulation	Bringing focus back to homework after a brief distraction, like a text; or being able to transition from a preferred activity (like video games) to homework	Moving smoothly between cleaning tasks as each is completed	Anticipating the various steps required while working and moving onto the next step when one is finished

TABLE 9.1 Examples of executive functioning difficulties

(Continued)

	Task: completing homework	*Task: cleaning the bedroom*	*Task: finishing a long-term school project*
Task initiation: taking the initial step of beginning a task	Getting homework out and beginning to work on it	Moving through feelings of overwhelm to pick a starting point and begin	Starting on the project with enough time to complete it without procrastinating until the deadline is near
Cognitive flexibility: viewing situations from a variety of angles and looking for new and different solutions when problems arise	Problem solving if the homework is difficult to try to find a new solution or strategy	Choosing to discard certain items that no longer are used or necessary, even if they were useful at one time	Attempting new and different ways to complete the project if a planned strategy is ineffective
Task persistence: persevering through a process from beginning to end; important for longer, multi-step projects or tasks	Moving from one portion of homework to the next subject until all homework for the evening is complete	Completing all steps of the process from beginning to end	Maintaining motivation from start to finish, without abandoning it when the novelty of the project wears off

TABLE 9.1 (Cont.)

through executive functioning skills increase as kids get older; because of this, it may seem like they are managing well for a while and then when the expectations become more difficult, they may need additional support again.

Most neurodivergent people who struggle with executive functioning will have some level of difficulty throughout their lives. We want kids to understand themselves and how their brains function. Kids who are equipped with this knowledge are able to find environments that work for them, create supports around themselves to accommodate their areas of difficulty, and advocate when appropriate to ask for support.

Our approach as parents is gradual and structured, again relying on the scaffolding technique of being able to provide support and remove it, little by little, as our kids become more independent. It is easy to become frustrated with our kids when they have trouble with executive functioning. Reminding ourselves that our kids want to do well and, if they aren't able to do well, it is generally because they don't have the skills necessary to be independent with them yet. Things that seem intuitive to us as adults may require more explicit (and repeated) instruction to our neurodivergent kids.

Skill-Building Is Not Behaviorism

There is a lot of talk in the neurodiversity community about what strategies are most effective to help neurodivergent people. There is the camp that looks to behaviorism to change how neurodivergent kids respond to the world. Applied behavioral analysis (ABA) is considered the "gold standard" in treating autistic individuals to learn "pro-social" behaviors, however, autistic adults who've experienced ABA talk about the trauma they've endured through this therapy. They often feel manipulated into being compliant and are taught their instinctual ways of doing things and being themselves are "wrong," while compliance with authority figures is emphasized. Cognitive-behavioral therapy provided without a neurodiversity-affirming framework teaches neurodivergent people, like ADHDers, that their executive functioning struggles are something they should be able to think their way out of.

There is some benefit in taking some aspects of certain behavioral techniques to support neurodivergent kids. For example, psychoeducation on how thoughts, feelings, and behaviors are related is directly pulled from cognitive-behavioral therapy. However, teaching twice-exceptional kids the theory behind the methods so they are empowered to build their own awareness and make choices about how to change is much different than using cognitive-behavioral techniques to push kids toward compliance. Neurodivergent kids are susceptible to bullying and other types of traumatization based on harmful relationships. Telling a kid who has been bullied that they are "mind reading" (a common "irrational belief" discussed in cognitive-behavioral therapy) when they predict that kids don't like them and will exclude them is denying their lived experiences. We need to give them the tools they need for success while building their sense of self-efficacy, rather than undermining it.

While some of the techniques in this section (and others) may pull from some types of behaviorally based therapies, they are framed in a way that is collaborative rather than manipulative. Kids are encouraged to make attempts to change the situations that are causing them distress, are validated even when their strategies fail, and given agency within their lives. We are equipping them to successfully navigate the world in a way that fits their neurodiversity.

Trusting the Process

When we work to teach our kids to develop executive functioning skills, we are working to create second-order change. While first-order change is surface-level change; second-order change transforms the system. For example, a child who has trouble remembering to bring home their instrument from band to practice may benefit from first-order change in the short term. If they aren't able to remember on their own, a parent might send a text message to remind them or set a punishment/reward system for remembering to bring it home or not. There is little to no change in the overall system, and the child will probably continue to struggle with remembering to bring home their instrument without these external forces. Parents and teachers may try to come up with new methods for reminders. The child continues to be dependent on the system for support.

Second-order change occurs when the roles are upended and the entire system shifts. We set the stage for second-order change through awareness, communication, and constant reevaluation of what is or isn't working. To see second-order change in the example above, the child has to begin to realize the power they have over their own successes and failures. They have to learn that they are accountable for their actions and, if just remembering to bring home their instrument isn't working, they can identify the steps necessary to solve the problem. Perhaps they develop an end-of-day routine and integrate it into that plan, or they decide to set a system that will alert them to double-check that they have their instrument. The second-order change is visible in the shift in communication and relationship style with the people who had been doing the heavy lifting to manage the child's executive functioning skills. The weight is shifted to the child, perhaps slowly, but consistently.

This process may be long, especially for some of our neurodivergent kids who struggle with understanding the big picture of why some things that are taking place today are so important for what is going to happen in the future. Some of them don't see the value in the skills we know they'll need for success as they get older. Perhaps you might fall into the same routines and roles within your relationship with your child, but the more you shift the power back to them, the more likely you are to gradually see that second-order change occur. Gradual development of these skills might be a long road, but note every bit of progress and trust that those bits of progress will accumulate to help your child grow into a confident and independent adult.

Leveraging Strengths

Many of our twice-exceptional children have internalized messages of ableism and feelings of being lazy or unmotivated based on their struggles with executive functioning skills. Grades suffer due to missing work, anxiety builds because of lack of organization, and the refrain about how they aren't "performing up to their potential" has often ingrained itself into their psyche. Taking the time to build executive functioning skills requires overcoming these negative self-beliefs to attempt to make changes.

In addition to hearing positive messages from you, their parent, to support their attempts, building executive functioning skills from a strengths-based approach is key. The easiest way to do this is to begin the process described in this chapter in an area where a child is motivated already. Dr. Matt Zakreski is a psychologist specializing in gifted individuals and makes the point about using a starting point of a child's strengths to build executive functioning skills on episode 76 of *The Neurodiversity Podcast*.

> If we were going to have you work on exercises and techniques to develop more executive functioning, it's easier to do it within the bounds of something you're already good at and something you enjoy rather than having you do it in something you dislike and struggle with. But, this is what we traditionally do at school. It's like, "Hey, Billy, we know you don't like math. I'm going to ask you to organize yourself better in math." He's already upset or unhappy being in math class. We're asking him to work on a difficult, challenging skill within the bounds of something that doesn't feel good.[1]

One twice-exceptional high school client was aware that executive functioning was an area of difficulty; his passion was music, but he noted he was even struggling with task initiation and managing his time to pursue his passion. Instead of immediately beginning to work on building executive functioning skills related to an area where he is already lacking feelings of self-efficacy, we began the process of building executive functioning skills related to a task he enjoyed – composing music – to help him learn the skills, which he was then able to generalize to other areas of his life where he wasn't as intrinsically motivated.

Accommodating Is Not Enabling

"Shouldn't they just be able to do this on their own?" "Is it fair that they get this help and other kids don't?" "Am I enabling my child and causing them to be dependent on me/the accommodations?"

It can feel frustrating to be offering accommodations to bright kids who, due to their uneven development, seem like they *should* be able to do these things on their own. It can be tempting to step away, hands in the air, and tell kids they are on their own. It can also feel paralyzing to know that you are offering help that may be too much. How do we find the "just right" amount of support and accommodations for our kids?

The best way I've found to handle this is to bring kids into the conversation. When our kids are aware of the accommodations that are provided, why they are provided, what the next steps toward independence are, and are involved in the process of establishing the accommodations that work for them, we are no longer enabling them. We are coaching them, guiding them, and facilitating the second-order change we need to move them toward independence.

Finding the Balance of Skill Building and Accommodations

I understand the difficulty that parents have when their kids can't seem to manage simple tasks. Parents get frustrated, and there may be resistance to putting accommodations in place. One client was in high school and had significant struggles with working memory and organization. This manifested in an inability to recall how his mother wanted him to load the dishwasher. He was generally compliant about loading the dishwasher when he got home from school (an alert on his phone helped him remember to do so), but his mother felt frustrated when certain items were placed in arrangements that would prevent them from being cleaned in the dishwasher. To her, this was a simple task and should just require a bit more effort from her son; if he "cared," he would not rush through the chore, taking time to put the items in the places she had taught him.

When I'm working with families, I try to find the right questions to ask to solve a problem. Is investigating whether this teen was just unmotivated to put forth effort (or worse, hoping if he kept doing it wrong he wouldn't have to keep doing it?) the most important answer to solve this problem? It is unlikely that we will ever find the real answer. However, if we give him the benefit of the doubt and assume he is doing the best he can with the skills he has, we move the conversation from "Why is this happening?" to "How do we fix it?" What are the practical tools he needs to accommodate his difficulty with placing the dishes in the right place? Instead of frequent auditory reminders (or lectures), we decided to provide a tool he could use as a reference in order to build independence. The next time the dishwasher needed to be loaded, his mom helped and, when they were done, the son took a photo of the correctly loaded dishwasher and created an album on his phone so it would always be accessible. We found a workaround to solve the problem, avoided the power struggle of trying to determine if he was just being "lazy," and gave him an opportunity to see how he can independently create and implement accommodations.

Many kids who struggle with executive functioning have a hard time with getting work completed and turned in on time. A blessing and a curse for many families is the online portal that provides updates from teachers about what assignments are turned in or missing. The blessing part of it is the ability to quickly access records and use it as an accountability tool. The flip side is that it encourages parents to act as the middleman or the enforcer and can quickly turn into a tool that takes away kids' autonomy and can lead to learned helplessness.

During the pandemic, one middle school client was struggling with completing work through his virtual school. It was third quarter and the ups and downs of an unusual school year were taking their toll. As a gifted/ADHD student, he was struggling with work completion and getting things turned in on time. Completing work on the computer was a huge temptation for him and he struggled to resist heading to watch online videos or to his favorite online game platform when he was supposed to be doing homework.

As this situation snowballed, his mom talked about her frustration during one of our sessions. He didn't care for being "nagged," so we were brainstorming some ideas to help him become more independent. When his parents would sit at the computer and go through each of his classes with him, asking about assignments, it would frequently become an argument. His mom suggested that she was willing to go through the classes and highlight the missing assignments for him and then he could go through the list to double check them or let her know what was happening with them. While helpful, I worried that this was letting her tween son off the hook too easily. If we're using the portal as a tool, he should be the one to check his assignments, print off the list and show it to his parents for accountability, and ask for help, if it was needed. When his mom offered to check the work for him and give him the list, we were moving away from independence; if he didn't want to sit with his parents and have their help to go through it, the expectation needed to be that he would need to increase his level of responsibility.

The questions to ask ourselves as we work to support our kids and scaffold their executive functioning skills are:

◆ What is the "just right" amount of support they need that doesn't lead to learned helplessness (too much support) or frustration/failure (too little support)?
◆ What tools can our kids use on their own to accommodate their difficulties (like the portal, reminders on a phone, etc.)?
◆ What are the next incremental steps our kids need to develop independence?

Thinking like a Scientist to Build Executive Functioning Skills

Twice-exceptional kids are logical thinkers; they often thrive when they are looking for patterns, collecting data, and solving problems. Harnessing this as a way to improve their executive functioning skills (or other skills you'd like to help them build) is a way to put them in charge of skill building. Kids are introduced at a young age to the scientific method at school. We can use this framework as a way to gather data, test new strategies, and develop awareness surrounding executive functioning skills. Essentially, what we are doing with this intervention is helping kids to identify a problem, create a hypothesis, and test the hypothesis. They are in charge, and it moves us away from the position of the person who passes judgment on whether they succeed or fail. It also allows us to ask neutral questions and offers them the opportunity to try new strategies. It also encourages the constant reevaluation – what's working and what isn't? – of skills and emphasizes that growth is a constant process and is never finished.

Kids can utilize this strategy from a young age, and you can easily tweak or modify it based on their ability. When you are ready to try this strategy with your child, start it out with an observation. "I notice that you are having a hard time with getting ready for school in the mornings." Ask for their insight into any causes or obstacles that might be causing difficulty in the area. Your role in this situation is to guide a conversation while letting them be the experts on their own lives. Offer observations and ask clarifying questions, but try to refrain from offering your interpretation of why the problem exists. Eventually, offer the suggestion of trying a new strategy to see if it helps the problem. "Let's experiment and try to collect some data to see if we can find a strategy that might be more helpful than what we're doing."

Steps to Use the Scientific Method to Build Executive Functioning Skills

Step One: Define the Problem
Brainstorm with your child about how they view the problem. Jot down the ideas. Be specific with the possible factors that are influencing the situation. We'll want to narrow down the problem to something specific so we can find actionable steps to take in the next phases of this strategy. Instead of identifying the problem as something broad and vague ("I'm too disorganized"), try to isolate a specific skill that is lagging ("I have trouble remembering to bring home all of my materials for my homework").

Step Two: Create a Hypothesis
Come up with several possible hypotheses that could potentially improve the area where your child is struggling. Encourage them to come up with some, and don't worry if they are a bit off the wall. Offer your own possible hypotheses, too. Once you have

a list of several hypotheses, let your child choose the one they think they would like to try as a strategy. Frame your hypothesis as an "if–then" statement. *If* this happens, *then* this will happen.

Step Three: Develop a Method

Define the method that will be used to test the hypothesis your child has chosen. What steps will you take to test your hypothesis? Are there certain materials you will need? How long will you conduct your experiment – a day, a week, a month? How frequently will you check in on the progress? What will you use to measure success?

Step Four: Collect Data

Let your child use their creativity to determine how they want to collect their data. Will they use a chart on paper, create an online spreadsheet, move paper clips from one side of a bookmark to the other, or make tally marks an index card? I've had kids create bracelets and keychains with beads to track frequency of behaviors throughout the day. Because your child is the one who is measuring their data, letting them create the plan for collecting the data is important.

It is vital that your child is the one who is collecting their own data. Make sure that the data collection isn't based on an adult's assessment of their success or failure. If your child is working to try to improve their response inhibition by reducing the number of times they call out in class, we want them to self-assess this. Having a teacher report back their assessment of progress might be tempting for both you and the teacher, however, when we remove the opportunity for independence, we are teaching our kids that they aren't able to be responsible for their own growth and change. Communication with and feedback from the school are important, however, this process needs to belong to your child.

Step Five: Analyze the Data

After the predetermined interval of time, check in with your child about their progress. Frequent communication and check-ins may be necessary and beneficial, depending on your child's level of independence with this task and it may be helpful to be flexible with what those time intervals are. You might be checking in with them anywhere from a few times a day to only once every one or two weeks.

As your child guides you through their data, ask them about what patterns they notice. Prompt them to make observations about the data. Ask a lot of questions during this analysis step: Did it appear that the strategy they were implementing influenced their performance, either positively or negatively? Were there any obstacles to implementing the strategy they didn't expect? Was the tracking system effective, or does it seem that tracking a different piece of data might be more useful? Once you have enough data to make some decisions, you're ready for the final step of the process.

Step Six: Evaluate the Information and Make Changes

After analyzing the data, your child has the chance to evaluate the information gathered. As they judge the effectiveness of the strategy, together you can decide if the strategy is useful enough to continue or if it needs to be tweaked. Is the data collection helpful in maintaining the strategy or is there enough awareness to continue to build the skill without the data collecting step? Should you continue to work on this skill or find a different one to address?

This decision-making process is where our kids have the opportunity to self-reflect. Offer your observations but try to let them come to their own conclusions. Whether you feel the process was effective or not, try to allow them to be their own judge. The overarching goal within this entire process is not actually the skill they are working on building, but the awareness they can develop about how to develop an idea for a strategy, try it out for a while, and then determine whether or not it was effective.

Thinking like a Scientist Case Study: Jevan

Jevan is struggling with managing his time in the mornings before school. Task initiation and sustained attention are obstacles, and the last few minutes before the bus arrives usually result in a panicked rush to get out the door in varying stages of readiness. The result of this mad race to get to the bus on time is a variety of forgotten materials and assignments at home which his parents often feel compelled to bring to school to rescue him. In the past, they family has tried to vary the routine by changing the sequence of responsibilities, which sometimes works for a very brief amount of time, but generally, Jevan's parents end up taking turns prodding him along in the mornings and lecturing him on the importance of timeliness and responsibility.

In order to facilitate second-order change, Jevan and his family need to shift the responsibility and awareness toward Jevan. In order to use the Thinking like a Scientist strategy, they sit down and develop a plan to walk through the steps.

Step One: Define the Problem

Mom: Jevan, Dad and I have noticed that the morning routines have really been difficult. We want to take a little time to have a family meeting about what is happening and how we might be able to improve the morning routines. What are some of the things you notice about the mornings?

Jevan: I dunno. I guess mornings are kind of stressful.

Dad: You're right – Mom and I get stressed, too, which I'm sure you can tell when we get frustrated and raise our voices or ground you from electronics for the day. I'm wondering which specific parts of the morning are stressful to you?

Jevan: Getting up when I'm tired is hard. And when I can't find something I need to bring to school in the morning, it throws me off-track.

Mom: I agree that getting up and going seems to be hard for you. I also notice that it is hard for you to choose what you want to eat for breakfast, and that slows things down.

Dad: I think we should try to come up with a plan to improve the mornings. I'm thinking we can frame it like it is a science experiment. Let's choose one of the stressful parts of the morning, come up with a hypothesis about one idea to make them go more smoothly, and then collect some data to see if it makes things better. Are you open to that idea?

Jevan: What if the hypothesis doesn't work? Do I get in trouble?

Dad: No, Jevan, there aren't any punishments with this. As a matter of fact, I think you should be the one who collects the data and decides if the strategy is helping or not. This is really just to help you and us feel better about the morning routines. Let's narrow it down to one thing that we might be able to try. We want it to be something that we can track or measure in some way, too.

Jevan: So, what do I get if I my hypothesis *does* work?

Mom: There isn't anything to earn with this either, other than things running more smoothly. We'll all feel more relaxed and won't have to so stressed out to start our days. So, any ideas?

Jevan: Well, one thing that might be kind of easy to change is whether or not I have my stuff ready and don't have to look around for things every morning.

Mom: Okay, that's a good starting point. Let's come up with a hypothesis about what might help this go more smoothly. The obvious thing that comes to my mind is making sure to get everything together before you go to bed so it is ready to go. Is there another idea you can think of?

Jevan: That might help. I think part of the other confusing part of getting my materials together in the mornings is when I can't remember what day it is. Like, do I have to bring my clarinet to school, or do I need my gym clothes, do I need to pack my lunch or buy, or remembering if I brought my laptop home the night before? It isn't the same stuff I have to get together every morning. But, getting everything together at night might mean this is easier.

Dad: I notice sometimes your stuff gets spread out through the house, too. Having a single place to keep everything might be helpful.

Mom: Okay, I hear several ideas. We could create a hypothesis and method to try to track whether getting things together the night before helps the morning routine. We could do something about trying to manage the changes in schedule to know what days certain materials are needed. Or, we could try to come up with an organized space that would allow you to have everything in one area. What do you think would be best?

Jevan: I think if I try to focus on getting my materials together the night before school, it would help with remembering what items I need based on the day because I'd have enough time to figure it out and would also mean things are more organized.

Step Two: Create a Hypothesis

Dad: Okay, so let's frame this as a hypothesis with an *if–then* sentence. So, *if* we do this, *then* this will happen. Let's brainstorm a few and then decide which one is best. I'll jot them down so we don't forget them.

Mom: Here's an idea. If Jevan gets his school stuff together at night, then he won't be late for the bus in the morning.

Jevan: If I set a routine to get all my school stuff together at night, then the mornings will feel calmer. Or, if I set an alarm to get my stuff together at night, then I won't have to rush to get things together in the morning.

Dad: If we use a chart or calendar to list what Jevan needs to get together in the evenings, then everything will already be ready in the morning before school. Any other hypotheses we can come up with? Or do we want to choose one of these?

Jevan: I think I like the idea of trying to set the alarm to remind me to get my stuff together because I'll probably just forget to do it. But, I might need to make a chart, too, so I can remember everything.

Dad: We can add the chart as part of our method if we want. So, we agree on the hypothesis, "If I set an alarm to get my school stuff together at night, then I won't have to rush to get things together in the morning," right?

Mom: Sounds good to me.

Jevan: Okay.

Step Three: Develop a Method

Mom: Okay, so the next part is coming up with a plan or the method that we want to use. We're going to have to collect some data, so we need to include some way of tracking our information. Also, we'll want to be really specific with the plan so we know exactly what to do and can see what works and what doesn't.

Dad: Okay, Jevan. You said you wanted to use an alarm to remind yourself to get your materials ready for school. What alarm do you want to use and what time do you think it should be set?

Jevan: I could use my phone, or I could use my watch. But sometimes I forget to wear my watch. My phone is pretty much always around. And I start getting ready for bed at 8, so maybe at that time.

Mom: I wonder if it might be a good idea to do it slightly earlier than 8:00 because we don't want it to become a problem to try to do it right at bedtime, either.

Jevan: 7:50?

Dad: I think 7:50 sounds like a good time to try. We can adjust it later when we evaluate our progress and adjust it if we need to. So, you're going to use your phone to set an alarm for 7:50 to take a few minutes to get your supplies together for school the next day? Okay, so do we want to create a chart for reference, too? What type of a chart or calendar do you want to use?

Jevan: Maybe we can print one out and I can keep it in the kitchen near my backpack.

Mom: That would be fine. Do you want it to be just a list or a calendar? Is it going to be something you want to write on or just look at for reference?

Jevan: Probably a calendar with a list for each day of the week.

Dad: Here are the steps I have for our method: 1. Jevan is going to set an alarm for 7:50 on his phone for school nights to remind him to get his stuff for school together. 2. We will create a weekly calendar with a list of items needed for school each day and keep it near Jevan's backpack as a reference. 3. We'll track whether the alarm and calendar work and how smoothly the next morning goes.

Mom: And we need to decide how long we want to try this before we check back in to see if it is working.

Jevan: One week?

Mom: I think one week is a good trial period to see how things are going and check back in.

Jevan: Okay.

Step Four: Collect Data

Dad, Mom, and Jevan create a tracking sheet for Jevan to use. It ends up looking like this:

	Monday	Tuesday	Wednesday	Thursday	Friday
Did I get my materials together when my alarm went off at 7:50?	☐ Yes, by myself ☐ Yes, with parent reminder(s) ☐ No, I didn't get it done	☐ Yes, by myself ☐ Yes, with parent reminder(s) ☐ No, I didn't get it done	☐ Yes, by myself ☐ Yes, with parent reminder(s) ☐ No, I didn't get it done	☐ Yes, by myself ☐ Yes, with parent reminder(s) ☐ No, I didn't get it done	☐ Yes, by myself ☐ Yes, with parent reminder(s) ☐ No, I didn't get it done
Was I able to find all of my materials?	☐ Yes ☐ No	☐ Yes ☐ No	☐ Yes ☐ No	☐ Yes ☐ No	☐ Yes ☐ No
What was the stress level while getting ready the next morning?	☐ 5 (Easy breezy) ☐ 4 (Pretty good) ☐ 3 (Okay) ☐ 2 (Kind of rushed) ☐ 1 (Almost missed the bus/missed the bus)	☐ 5 (Easy breezy) ☐ 4 (Pretty good) ☐ 3 (Okay) ☐ 2 (Kind of rushed) ☐ 1 (Almost missed the bus/missed the bus)	☐ 5 (Easy breezy) ☐ 4 (Pretty good) ☐ 3 (Okay) ☐ 2 (Kind of rushed) ☐ 1 (Almost missed the bus/missed the bus)	☐ 5 (Easy breezy) ☐ 4 (Pretty good) ☐ 3 (Okay) ☐ 2 (Kind of rushed) ☐ 1 (Almost missed the bus/missed the bus)	☐ 5 (Easy breezy) ☐ 4 (Pretty good) ☐ 3 (Okay) ☐ 2 (Kind of rushed) ☐ 1 (Almost missed the bus/missed the bus)

Other notes?

Step Five: Analyze the Data

After a week, Jevan's data collecting sheet looks like this:

	Monday	Tuesday	Wednesday	Thursday	Friday
Did I get my materials together when my alarm went off at 7:50 the night before?	☑ Yes, by myself ☐ Yes, with parent reminder(s) ☐ No, I didn't get it done	☐ Yes, by myself ☐ Yes, with parent reminder(s) ☑ No, I didn't get it done	☐ Yes, by myself ☑ Yes, with parent reminder(s) ☐ No, I didn't get it done	☐ Yes, by myself ☑ Yes, with parent reminder(s) ☐ No, I didn't get it done	☑ Yes, by myself ☐ Yes, with parent reminder(s) ☐ No, I didn't get it done
Was I able to find all of my materials?	☑ Yes ☐ No	☐ Yes ☑ No	☑ Yes ☐ No	☐ Yes ☑ No	☑ Yes ☐ No
What was the stress level while getting ready the next morning?	☐ 5 (Easy breezy) ☑ 4 (Mostly calm) ☐ 3 (Okay) ☐ 2 (Kind of rushed) ☐ 1 (Almost missed the bus/missed the bus)	☐ 5 (Easy breezy) ☐ 4 (Mostly calm) ☐ 3 (Okay) ☐ 2 (Kind of rushed) ☑ 1 (Almost missed the bus/missed the bus)	☐ 5 (Easy breezy) ☐ 4 (Mostly calm) ☑ 3 (Okay) ☐ 2 (Kind of rushed) ☐ 1 (Almost missed the bus/missed the bus)	☐ 5 (Easy breezy) ☑ 4 (Mostly calm) ☐ 3 (Okay) ☐ 2 (Kind of rushed) ☐ 1 (Almost missed the bus/missed the bus)	☑ 5 (Easy breezy) ☐ 4 (Mostly calm) ☐ 3 (Okay) ☐ 2 (Kind of rushed) ☐ 1 (Almost missed the bus/missed the bus)
Other notes?	*Bedtime rushed because took a long time to find everything*	*Baseball practice Monday night; not enough time*	*Distracted in the morning*		*Best day! Ready early*

Jevan's parents sit down together over the weekend to look over the chart together. They've also had occasional conversations throughout the week regarding using the chart and the plan.

Dad: Let's look for some patterns and see what we learned over the week about what worked and what didn't work. What do you notice, Jevan?

Jevan: I think the week went well. Most of the mornings were okay or better. But, I know it was hard to do some of the nights because I didn't want to stop what I was doing to get everything together.

Mom: I agree that things were easier this week, overall. I'm really proud of how well you did.

Dad: What else do you notice about the data we collected? Or anything about the process that you weren't expecting?

Jevan: I liked having the calendar for a reference to see what I needed. I didn't feel like I needed to keep going over in my head what I already had and what I needed to remember. It made getting everything together quicker.

Mom: Was there anything you were expecting to work but didn't?

Jevan: I thought the alarm on my phone would work really well, but you ended up reminding me anyway. I think I can do it if you give me the chance to try.

Dad: Okay, maybe we can talk about when specifically you want us to remind you or not when we see what changes we should make.

Step Six: Evaluate the Information and Make Changes

Mom: Okay, now that we've looked over the data, we're ready to judge how things went and decide what changes we should make. First, do we think this was helpful?

Jevan: Yeah, I think it was better.

Dad: So, should we keep doing the same thing? Or do we want to make some changes? We could keep trying to use this strategy and come up with a totally different area to collect data.

Mom: I feel like this was a really good start and I'd love to keep working on this to make it go even more smoothly before we switch to something else. Especially with helping to build your independence so Dad and I don't have to double check and get you going to get things together at night. That's my two cents. Unless there is something you really want to work on that is different.

Jevan: I think I could keep working on this one. I want to try to figure out how to do it on my own, too. I think I can do it by myself, but you guys remind me before I have a chance to get it finished on my own.

Dad: I'm okay with figuring something out, but I think we should collect some data on that. Should we tweak the strategy and how you are reminded with your phone? I'm thinking maybe an alarm a few minutes before the actual alarm goes off as a warning so you can get ready? Do you want Mom or me to remind you after a certain amount of time?

Jevan: So, like an alarm at 7:47 and then another alarm at 7:50? Maybe I'll add a third alarm at 7:52 as a final warning. Maybe you can give me a reminder at 7:58?

Mom: Okay, I think we can give that a try. Should we use the same tracking chart and just add a new row for what time you got started?

Jevan: That's a good idea.

Dad: Okay, so I think I hear a new hypothesis. If Jevan adds a warning alarm and a reminder alarm, then he will start getting his school stuff together without reminders from Mom or Dad. How does that sound?

Jevan: Sounds good to me!

Jevan and his family continue to work through the scientific process and build the skills needed to support his executive functioning difficulties. Sometimes, kids may want to switch gears completely and try a new topic to build skills around. Letting your child have as much control as possible to improve their habits is key. Completing this activity has multiple goals and positive outcomes. In addition to facilitating effective and solution-focused communication within families, it helps to develop strategies that make the day-to-day responsibilities and expectations more manageable. It also teaches kids that they can create new habits and behaviors, or use the tools available as accommodations to improve their overall success for daily tasks.

Helping Resistant Kids

There may be kids who are resistant to any type of strategy. This may be due to learned helplessness – a feeling that they have no ability to change the world or the way they interact with it. Perhaps they experience overwhelming demand avoidance (see p. 44). Or some kids may be open to trying to find a solution for a problem, but immediately forget or don't follow through. Others may also be very direct with their unwillingness to change; they don't see a problem or don't see the value in changing.

In any of these situations, we can continue to support our neurodivergent kids by breaking down the scaffolding into smaller and more discrete steps to build confidence. For example, the tracking of data on its own can be the goal. "If I use a spreadsheet on my phone, I can collect data about my mood on a daily basis," could be a basic goal to help build self-efficacy that a child *can* build their awareness and work toward improving their skills.

We can honor kids' experiences and meet them where they are. I won't lie to you and pretend this is a quick fix. This process is often slow. The internalized messages our kids have learned about themselves from being in academic settings that are not a good fit for them, and the ableist messages they've received from society about what they should be and how they should behave, are difficult to unwind. However, recognizing that starting now, at whatever point they are at, and giving them the tools to figure out what works for them is powerful and will stay with them for a lifetime.

Chapter Reflection

- ◆ What areas of executive functioning are a strength for your child? Which are areas of struggle?
- ◆ In what areas might your child be able to make some preliminary changes to build self-efficacy surrounding supporting their executive functioning struggles?

◆ Do you tend to gravitate toward finding the solutions for your child without allowing them to attempt their own solutions? How does that impact your relationship with your child?

Note

1. Zakreski, M. (2021, January 27). A neurodiversity framework for gifted and 2e [Audio blog interview]. Retrieved from https://neurodiversitypodcast.com/home/2021/1/26/episode-76-supporting-gifted-amp-2e-people-using-a-neurodiversity-framework

10

Skill #4 – Effective Social Communication

Our twice-exceptional kids should understand the importance of communication, know the methods that are most useful to them for communicating with others, and recognize how communication impacts their relationships with others. Effective social communication is the key to healthy relationships. While writing this book, I originally planned to include separate chapters for effective communication and building social relationships with peers, but as I worked on writing them, I realized how intertwined the two are. I can't write about building positive social relationships without addressing communication and vice versa. Ultimately, it made the most sense to combine the two topics. If we can help kids develop effective communication strategies, they'll be able to implement them to create healthy relationships with others.

To foster a neurodiversity-affirming framework to support communication for our twice-exceptional kids, we have to honor how our kids naturally communicate. We have to understand the type of connection they are seeking by communicating. Sometimes when working with my clients, I feel like I am acting as an interpreter between neurodivergent and neurotypical communication styles. Sometimes I'm helping parents understand

DOI: 10.4324/9781003237532-14

their children, sometimes helping kids understand their parents. Other times, I'm helping kids find ways to better communicate with their friends at school. Anywhere there is a relationship, it relies on communication.

Self-advocacy was addressed as its own unique skill because of its importance, and you'll find that many of the strategies and topics discussed here are reliant on some level of self-advocacy to improve most situations. We can help our kids come up with more specific communication tools that will help with self-advocacy efforts and improve their relationships in general. This chapter will discuss how to help your child learn to communicate with people in various roles and in varied situations to grow their independence. There are also ideas for how you can support their neurodivergent style of communication.

As you begin supporting your child to build more effective communication strategies, try to model the type of communication that you'd like them to use. Keep a neutral tone of voice and ask lots of clarifying questions. Operate from a place where you are presuming competence and recognizing that if your child is struggling it isn't that they *can't* or *won't*; they simply need additional tools or support right now while they build their independence toward the skill. If a conversation begins spiraling toward emotional dysregulation or gets stuck and is no longer making any progress, acknowledge the fact that it is no longer a helpful conversation and make a decision to come back to it later.

Perspective Taking

A key component to communication is perspective taking. Anticipating what another person is thinking or what they might do is how we determine how we will respond. Some of us are intuitive perspective takers; we can innately understand what others are thinking or feeling without much effort. It doesn't always come naturally to others. Twice-exceptional kids might be prone to overthinking all the different possibilities that could be going through someone's mind and be unable to settle on what is the most likely. Some may fear making a guess because it might be wrong; it feels safer to say or do nothing instead. Other neurodivergent kids have a difficult time imagining what others are thinking at all. Autistic individuals, who often thrive on finding patterns and evidence to support their theories, can feel overwhelmed when asked to imagine what is going through another person's mind.

Understanding Empathy

There is a connection between perspective taking and empathy. Some people might suggest they are the same thing. However, I prefer to differentiate the two because "lack of empathy" is frequently misunderstood and weaponized against neurodivergent (usually) autistic people. This stems from a misunderstanding of the various components of empathy.

Empathy can be broken into two parts. The first type of empathy is cognitive empathy. This is most closely related to perspective taking and is sometimes called "theory of mind." Cognitive empathy requires someone to anticipate what someone else is thinking. I explain this concept to clients with this example: "If someone had a thought bubble above their head, what would be in it?" Interpreting this requires a lot of contextualization of the situation and making inferences based on a person's nonverbal communication. Some neurodivergent people are extremely concrete, and making these types of assumptions can be difficult.

Another obstacle that some neurodivergent individuals might face in this situation is that while they might understand what the other person is thinking, they may be uncertain about how to respond or how to verbalize their understanding of the situation. Or they may have a difficult time expressing it because it elicits such strong emotions in themselves, making it difficult to process and communicate.

The second type of empathy is referred to as affective empathy. Affective empathy is the ability to connect and feel with another person. If somebody knows what emotions another person is feeling, they can connect with that emotion and feel it within themselves alongside the other person. Affective empathy moves us toward compassionate acts to help others, to alleviate their uncomfortable emotions. Someone who struggles with guessing someone else's thoughts or emotions (cognitive empathy) can still have an intense understanding of another's emotions and be able to connect through those shared feelings (affective empathy).

Coaching Perspective Taking

Kids can become more confident in perspective taking and improve this skill with support. Here are some ideas to help scaffold your child toward building their ability to understand others' perspectives.

♦ When you are talking to your child, find ways to narrate your thought process to them. This can help them see the different types of perspectives people might have in various situations and help them adjust their communication because they aren't having to guess what you're thinking. "I'm a little worried about trying to get everything finished tonight, so I'm thinking about all of the things we have to do, estimate how much time they'll take, and prioritize what is most important. I can't really see how we're going to get everything finished that we want to do, so I know we'll have to cut one or two things out, but it is stressful for me because everything is pretty important."

♦ Take opportunities to make inferences about movie and book characters, or people you observe while you are out. Create an inner dialogue for them, using context clues about what they might be thinking. Make remarks about the signs that give you the hints about what they might be thinking. If your child has a harder time creating their own inner dialogue for others, you could make it a game where you suggest two possible thoughts the person is having, and they have to guess which one they think is closer and back up their answer with their own observations.

♦ Encourage lots of question asking. If your child isn't sure what you mean by something or what your intent is, let them know it is okay to ask for clarification. This is also important in settings at school with teachers or peers. If your child struggles to interpret the intent behind someone's statement, asking, "Are you being serious or joking?" or "I'm not sure I understand what you mean," can avoid a lot of frustration.

◆ Help your child understand the nuances of communication, while validating their experiences that may cause difficulty. For example, one twice-exceptional client in high school understood cognitively that there was difference between a demand and a request, however, when communicating, had a hard time identifying whether it would come across as a demand or request because of his difficulties with social language. His parents would gently suggest different phraseology when a request came across as a demand.

Communicating with Peers

Neurodivergent people frequently prefer different communication styles than their peers. Sometimes this can be a benefit – for example, the divergent thinking and quick processing of some 2e kids leads them to be natural entertainers. But there are other reasons that this varied communication might hinder the development of friendships. The major factor in influencing how social connections develop is based on how we communicate with others, and our neurodivergent kids often communicate differently. The natural way our kids communicate isn't inherently "wrong," however, if it isn't helping them build the relationships they would like, we either need to help them adjust their communication or help them find people who communicate in the same way they do. While the list is not exhaustive, there are several reasons why twice-exceptional kids might struggle to communicate in a way that facilitates positive social relationships. If you notice your child is struggling with effective communication with their peers, assess whether any of these possible areas may be part of the area of concern.

Different Communication Styles

The problem: Neurodivergent kids' communication styles aren't always the same as their neurotypical peers. Some kids may have a hard time finding the right words to say, others might have a hard time identifying when they should stop talking. Some may prefer very straightforward language that doesn't beat around the bush, however, some recipients of this language might not understand or like this approach. Some of this communication (or miscommunication) may be directly related to someone's neurodivergence.

The solution: As with many of the topics associated with supporting our twice-exceptional kids, we want to presume competence. When twice-exceptional kids express the desire to communicate more effectively, but they are lacking the skills needed, we can coach them to learn the new skills. Explicit instruction about how others are noticing or interpreting our words can make a big difference for our kids. For example, when conducting support groups for neurodivergent kids, we talk about how to effectively communicate. I often use the example of how conversations should be like a ping-pong game – one person hitting the ball over the net and waiting for the other person to return it. (Of course, one of my very literal group participants pointed out that the goal of ping-pong is to hit the ball so the other person *can't* return it to you! I had to laugh, and he admitted that he understood the point of the analogy.) Role play and practice with scripting conversations can help alleviate the fear of saying the wrong thing until responses come more naturally. Making observations about communication in your daily life and noting what does and doesn't work can also help build awareness of the most effective strategies. And encourage your child to attempt to explain how they interpret certain situations and communication styles so you have a better understanding of how they perceive certain events.

Being a "Know-It-All" (aka Others-Oriented Perfectionism)

The problem: I'm not a fan of the phrase "know-it-all," because gifted kids often know *a lot* and want to share that information with people. However, there is a type of communication that can often hinder relationship building that makes kids come across as the unwelcome type of "know-it-all." It is based on others-oriented perfectionism.

Others-oriented perfectionism is exactly what it sounds like. It is a type of perfectionism that is directed outward toward others. It is the child who corrects the teacher, acts like a mini-adult with their peers, or can't pass up a chance to criticize their sibling. They often come across as bossy and struggle to work in groups because they believe their ideas are the best. They either insist on doing all the work themselves or get frustrated and ask to work independently because nobody else is doing it "right" (also known as the way *they* think it should be done).

Some others-oriented perfectionism is based on black-and-white thinking. The thinking seems to be, "There is a right way to do things, and a wrong way to do things, so why would anyone do them the wrong way?" Sometimes kids feel like correcting others is actually being helpful, even if it comes across in a negative manner. Others-oriented perfectionism can be a hard habit to break.

The solution: Awareness of others-oriented perfectionism is key to reducing its occurrence and impact in social relationships. In a small counseling group I facilitated for exceptionally gifted students, I had the kids complete a questionnaire to determine what type of perfectionist they were (the other two types are self-oriented and socially prescribed perfectionists). One of the kids gasped, and exclaimed this was "basically [his] entire personality" when he made the realization of how he was coming across to his friends. I'm not certain it stopped right away, but the awareness certainly helped.

Some basic healthy self-talk skills can be useful. Help kids recognize that millisecond pause before they offer their opinion to others and ask themselves a few questions before they speak. "Is it my responsibility to correct this person?" "Do they want my advice?" "Does it impact me directly?" Also, working to come up with some basic perspective taking can help. "I don't really like it when other kids my own age correct me; they probably won't like it if I correct them, either."

Finding Like-Minded Peers

The problem: Twice-exceptional kids have unique profiles of strengths and weaknesses. They also have divergent interests that may vary from the norm. Finding peers that can keep up with them intellectually, have similar interests, and a complementary communication style can be a little like finding a needle in a haystack. If a twice-exceptional kid is in a classroom with a bunch of kids who just "don't get them," no amount of building social skills is going to overcome that divide. Some 2e kids gravitate toward engaging with the adults, both because the adults are generally more gracious about any lagging social skills and because the adults are able to engage in topics that other same-aged peers may not find interesting. Others gravitate toward younger peers, because they get to fill the role of mentor and, again, younger kids are more forgiving of social differences.

Without opportunities to engage in healthy, productive social interactions, kids can lose confidence in their ability to interact in social situations. They may hesitate to approach peers or find themselves masking their natural social communication style in an effort to fit in, even if it doesn't fulfill their desire for a "real" connection.

The solution: Finding the opportunity for kids to connect with like-minded peers can require some creativity. One of the positive outcomes of so many things transitioning to online during the pandemic was the opportunity for creative problem-solving to help kids find ways to stay connected with others. For our twice-exceptional kids, this greatly broadens the pool of possible connections. I know kids who've started participating in Dungeons and Dragons games with kids from other countries, and online Pokémon games that span ages and states. If your child does better with in-person activities, look for opportunities in the community; try not to limit your search to certain age groups. Finding peers who are older or younger might be just what your child needs. The solution is *not* to try to force your child to participate in activities they aren't interested in with kids who don't get them for the sake of "socialization." If we're working to take a strengths-based approach and we put a socially anxious kid in an improv group to try to bring them out of their shell, at best they'll grin and bear it; at worst, we'll cause more anxiety and they'll internalize the message that they can't succeed in those environments even more.

Communicating Electronically

The problem: The usage of texting, instant messaging, emailing, and every other method of electronic communication has greatly changed the landscape of social communication for kids. On the one hand, it can be a blessing for our neurodivergent kids. Having the time to pause and craft a response rather than communicate verbally in real time can be a benefit, especially for those neurodivergent kids who deal with social anxiety. On the other hand, the lack of context in some forms of electronic communication can cause difficulties and misunderstandings. We've all been in the situation where we were reading a text or an email and questioned the intent of the sender, wondering if they are upset or if they are being sarcastic.

Just like the subtleties during in-person conversations, there are details through electronic communications that can imply certain meanings that may not be automatically understood. For example, how many of us typically use basic punctuation in text messages? The difference between a text message that says "no" versus one that says "no." for today's kids is vast. A period at the end of a single-word text message indicates an abrupt end to a conversation, and a member of Gen Z often interprets this as a signal that the sender may be upset. The code switching required for casual electronic communication and more formal writing done at school may be difficult for neurodivergent kids.

There are also hidden rules about contacting people electronically that neurodivergent kids may not recognize. For example, one client I worked with ran into difficulties because he didn't realize that, even though he had access to everyone in his class's email address, he shouldn't use those email addresses for personal communication without checking with the person first. A quick "Hey, is it okay for me to email you?"

can avoid a lot of confusion and difficulty. Or, adding people on social media that aren't people one knows personally can also cause not only communication issues, but safety concerns as well.

The solution: Just like offering guidance on verbal and nonverbal communication for in-person interactions, have conversations with your child about how to appropriately converse with people in virtual settings. The rules of reciprocal conversation still apply, and waiting for a response from someone, rather than barraging someone with multiple messages, is important. When your child enters the online world, whether their first interaction is texting with a phone, emailing through the school server, or messaging through the chat function of a game, having a clear conversation about what behaviors are acceptable and what boundaries are expected goes a long way. Having this in written form and occasionally revisiting and revising it as necessary can help clarify any confusion and offer the opportunity to talk about the reasons why certain norms exist with how we communicate with others.

Fostering Neurodivergent Social Relationships

The first factor that is important to consider when we discuss helping our kids build healthy and positive social relationships is recognizing that what might be best for our children isn't necessarily what society has taught us is the "appropriate" desired form of relationships. Neurodivergent kids' abilities and interests can drastically influence how they interact with their peers and other individuals in their lives. We want to respect our kids' autonomy while helping them build the skills they may not have developed independently. Breaking free from expectations requires a truly neurodiversity-affirming perspective.

Is it okay if your child gets along with and wants to spend time with older or younger individuals than themselves? What about if they prefer to read a book during lunch and recess rather than interact with their peers? Or, if most of their friendships are with people who they've met and solely interact with online? Any of these might be a fine fit for your child; the only way to know is to explore the topic with them directly. If they are feeling lonely and want to develop more friendships, we should find ways to foster that; however, we shouldn't try to force relationships on our child if they aren't dissatisfied with how things currently are.

There are a lot of reasons why twice-exceptional kids might struggle with developing friendships. Some of these are relational, some of them are environmental. Understanding why twice-exceptional kids might have a harder time than others developing positive social relationships and maintaining those friendships is important in order to help kids build better relationships.

If you recognize that your child is unhappy with their relationships, or has difficult interactions with others that cause additional distress, or lacks some of the skills needed to manage their relationships, we can help them learn some skills to overcome these obstacles. Using a collaborative approach helps your child develop at a pace that is appropriate for their abilities (which may be greatly asynchronous to their cognitive ability).

Conflict Resolution

Resolving conflicts is a key component to building healthy friendships and other relationships. Some twice-exceptional kids might have trouble with resolving conflicts because they have trouble regulating their emotions, they are very black-and-white in their thinking, or they are unable to admit when they are wrong. Bright kids are often natural debaters, using their wit and mastery of verbal communication to support their case. If one is always used to winning arguments, it can make it hard to back down from one that might not be won.

Sometimes, twice-exceptional kids describe the desire to make new or more friends, yet they have habits that lead to conflict or don't know how to compromise. For example, I often work with 2e kids who would like to play with other kids at recess. When we talk about what they would like to play, they have a single activity they are willing to do and if their peers want to do something else, they feel excluded. They refuse to compromise and join the other activity with their peers. I talk to kids about the choices they have (sometimes we list them on paper or a dry erase board) and try to explore the pros and cons of each option. We look for possible compromises, misunderstandings, or opportunities to come up with other new solutions. And, if the ultimate choice they make is that they'd prefer to do an activity on their own, we work through the emotions associated with that choice.

Twice-exceptional kids also need strategies to set and communicate healthy boundaries with their peers. Sometimes the desire to become friends with other kids is so great that kids will go to great lengths to accommodate their peers, even when they are doing something they either don't really want to do or know isn't the safest or best choice. One late-elementary client has been in a friendship with a peer who is extremely possessive of my client's time and very jealous whenever my client spends time with another friend. My client is uncomfortable with the situations, but has had trouble making friends in the past, so he is scared to lose this friend, even though he knows it isn't a healthy relationship. We're working on finding ways to set boundaries with this friend and say "no" when he makes requests that are unreasonable. Especially for kids who may not make and keep friends easily, the fear of a losing a friend causes them to be especially vulnerable to peer pressure.

The ability to set healthy boundaries begins with the parental relationship. If we are having an argument (or heated conversation) with our child and they would like to take a break and go to their room, do we allow them that time to cool off or do we tell them to stay so we can "finish the conversation"? We can respect our children's autonomy and personhood while still providing structure and boundaries within the familial unit. When kids know they are heard and respected at home, they are more likely to expect that in other relationships outside of the house.

Another strategy for our kids to develop to manage conflict resolution involves integrating dialectical thinking (also discussed in Chapter 8). As it relates to relationships, dialectical thinking involves recognizing that two seemingly opposite points of view can both be valid. Knowing that my perspective and your perspective, even if they are different, can both be true is necessary to be able to resolve conflicts within relationships effectively. Here are a few examples of some dialectical thinking applied to relationships:

- ◆ I knocked someone's belongings on the floor accidentally *and* I can be sorry that my actions caused it to happen.
- ◆ It can feel unfair that I don't get to have the same privileges as my older sister *and* I can understand why my parents set those boundaries.
- ◆ I can disagree with my group mates on what is the best idea for our project *and* I can compromise and let them have some input on how to complete it.

Finally, there will be times when our kids need to take responsibility for their actions and offer an apology. This can be hard for anyone, but neurodivergent kids might have a harder time than others, if they struggle with talking about emotions or self-regulation. I use the 5-Step Apology with my clients for several reasons. First, it provides a script for what is often an uncomfortable conversation that requires a significant amount of vulnerability. Also, it doesn't let kids get away with a rushed "Sorry" mumbled under their breath. It requires them to use some perspective taking and to identify a way to work toward making the situation better.

The 5-Step Apology isn't only for kids. When parents take the time to acknowledge their mistakes and model a thoughtful apology, we teach kids that it is okay to be imperfect and it is important to take action to repair relationships that are damaged by our actions, even if they are unintentional.

The 5-Step Apology

Step One: The Apology
This one is simple. Say "I'm sorry."

Step Two: The Reason
Tell why you are apologizing. What was the action that caused harm to another person?

Step Three: Perspective Taking
How do you believe this situation made the person feel? How could you tell?

Step Four: Preventing Recurrence
How will you make sure this situation doesn't happen again?

Step Five: Righting the Wrong
What will you do to "right the wrong" or make up for the situation that occurred?

Examples
  ◆ (1) I'm sorry (2) I yelled at you when you told me to do my homework. (3) I could tell you felt frustrated because you'd already asked me a bunch to get it done. (4) Next time, I'll start my homework before I start playing video games. (5) After I'm done with my homework, I'll do an extra chore.
  ◆ (1) I'm sorry (2) I lost the colored pencils you let me borrow. (3) You felt disappointed because you trusted me to use them and return them. (4) If you let me borrow something, I'll use it and return it right away, so it doesn't get lost. (5) I'm going to order you some new colored pencils to replace the ones I lost.
  ◆ (1) I'm sorry (2) I made you late to work this morning because I didn't get ready in time. (3) I know you felt worried about being late to work and upset that I didn't manage my time this morning. (4) Next time, I'll wake up earlier and avoid playing with my brother while we're getting ready. (5) I'm going to help you with whatever you need today after school.

Chapter Reflection

  ◆ When does your child communicate effectively? What situations are more difficult for them?

- ◆ How does your child experience and communicate cognitive and affective empathy?
- ◆ What are your expectations for your child's social relationships? Does that align with the current reality of their peer relationships?
- ◆ How does your child's communication style impact their social relationships?

11

Skill #5 – Self-Directed Motivation

You've been working with your child to develop their self-advocacy, executive functioning, emotional regulation, and social communication skills. Through each of these processes, we've worked to empower our kids and allow them to have a sense of agency. This sense of agency or autonomy is a necessary part of the process as they engage each skill because it means our kids are taking an active role in developing these skills. Small successes lead to gradual increases in self-efficacy, which helps increase their motivation. As that momentum leads to more successes, their motivation is stoked further. It is a virtuous cycle we hope to encourage.

We want our kids to experience success in order to help them move toward their goals and find their place in this world. Twice-exceptional kids are prone to experience situations they may interpret as failures. The strategies discussed in the previous chapters all work to emphasize the belief that process trumps product. We want our kids to know that, even if we might work toward something and have a setback, we shouldn't give up. The setbacks give us direction to know what steps to take next.

We need and want our kids to set attainable goals without needing a carrot dangled in front of them to entice them to keep moving. Being able to target a goal independently and move

DOI: 10.4324/9781003237532-15

toward it is the foundation for self-directed motivation. Some parents might feel their child is unmotivated, however, nobody is unmotivated. Society has trained us to view motivation through the lens of the activities society has deemed important. Someone who is labeled "unmotivated" may actually be very motivated … just not to work towards the goals that have been predetermined by social expectations. Parents need to ask themselves: Where do we see our kids' motivation? Are they are motivated to build with LEGO or play video games or text with their friends? Through this chapter, we'll discuss strategies to help twice-exceptional kids set specific goals, the benefits of making progress toward those goals, and how all of this can lead to self-directed motivation and, ultimately, self-actualization. We'll also discuss the various forms of intrinsic and extrinsic motivation. Helping kids understand how motivation influences even basic responsibilities can be helpful as they become more independent.

Executive functioning skills and emotional regulation skills are intricately tied to motivation. Future orientation is essentially an executive functioning skill, tied to awareness of time and prioritization of tasks. It is the ability to look toward the future and understand how today's actions influence what that future looks like. Seeing the big picture of how events are tied together in cause and effect is necessary to establish future orientation. The ability to tolerate mild emotional discomfort is also necessary for motivation because the steps required to reach a goal may include some tasks that aren't exciting or pleasant.

Motivation also relies on effort, and some neurodivergent kids have a hard time regulating their effort. Things that seem easy to others may be extremely difficult to them. Or they may have a hard time assessing the level of effort that is needed for a task. Motivation and effort are intertwined but are different constructs. Motivation is the desire to do something. We want the feeling of having the task accomplished or the end result of having it done. Effort is the action pushed forward by motivation. If motivation is the gas in the tank of the car; effort is the pressure we put on the gas pedal to make the car go. Twice-exceptional kids have extraordinary engines with a lot of horsepower. However, the nature of their asynchronous development and inconsistent executive functioning skills can make it difficult to reach the gas pedal. Having frequent conversations with your twice-exceptional child about motivation, effort, and responsibilities will help them gain an awareness of their own relationship to these constructs. Just like with the other skills discussed in this book, we want to continue to leverage their cognitive ability to increase self-awareness.

As parents who hope to be neurodiversity-affirming within their relationships with their children, we have to operate from a place of mutual trust. Doing so requires us to move at our kids' pace, recognize what is important to them, and support them toward their goals. This balance can be at odds with the structure of the world. Helping our kids develop self-directed motivation is done through open and honest conversations with our children about what works for them and how they see themselves fitting into the world.

Underachievement

In academic settings, twice-exceptional learners often face underachievement, meaning they aren't developing the skills or performing at the level that is expected for their ability, grade level, or age. Underachievement is the reason that many twice-exceptional learners are originally identified as 2e. Their compensatory skills no longer suffice, and they are struggling to achieve as expected. When twice-exceptional kids begin to underachieve, it can look like a lack of motivation. Caution should be used interpreting the reasons why a child appears to be losing motivation. We should first determine what might be getting in the way of expected achievement, like an underlying learning disability or an inability to organize their materials and tasks appropriately.

It is also important to note that twice-exceptional kids can be overachievers. Many kids who are neurodivergent are desperate to keep up their grades and will go to extreme lengths to maintain that level of achievement. The trouble with this is that, as they get older, the expectations in school or social situations continue to outpace their abilities. This leads to increased, and sometimes debilitating, stress and anxiety. "Gifted kid burnout" is a colloquial term used to describe the feeling of exhaustion from desperately trying to manage all of the expectations bright kids face during school; twice-exceptional learners (especially unidentified twice-exceptional learners) are especially prone to experiencing this type of burnout. Sometimes, kids will appear to abruptly transition from an overachiever to an underachiever; this can be a sign that the effort of compensating has become too much.

Let's be real: for some of our twice-exceptional learners, it is difficult to justify motivation for some tasks associated with school. Some of them might be academically ready to enter college when they begin high school (or earlier). Others might be jaded about school because they've been unsupported. They just can't see any reason to try. Most gifted kids are highly motivated to *learn*, they just aren't as motivated to do *school*. It is unfortunate that our educational system is a one-size-fits-most environment. Without both appropriate challenge *and* support, it is all too easy to extinguish any flicker of motivation a student might have.

When I talk to parents, almost every one of them states that they don't necessarily want their child to have straight A's; they just want to know that their child is trying to do well. Defining what motivation looks like, though, is subjective. Twice-exceptional kids often *are* trying, but the outcomes of their effort are inconsistent, muddled by the perception of others that they aren't "living up to their potential." Or they've internalized the message that they *can't* do the task that is expected, so they are reticent to try.

Communicating with kids about motivation and underachievement from a place of solution-focused compassion can help normalize their experiences and give them permission to express their feelings of frustration or vulnerability. If we want to work with kids to help them channel their motivation toward their goals, we need to believe them when they say they want to succeed and continue to scaffold the supports they need to be successful. Finding motivation for skills that are related to a specific task is also shown to use self-directed motivation.[1]

Intrinsic Motivation and the Truth about Rewards

While we would all love for our children to be intrinsically motivated about all of the things we deem important, we also know that isn't a reality. Let's be honest – very few of us are intrinsically motivated to do many of the things we do on a daily basis. Intrinsic motivation means that the activity itself is the reward. I'm intrinsically motivated to read, play board games with my kids, and (attempt to) teach myself to play the piano. While I love my work, and am motivated to help others, it isn't wholly intrinsically motivated. As much as we may love our jobs, without a paycheck, we'd need to find a new career.

Another way to look at motivation breaks intrinsic and extrinsic motivation into smaller components. Ryan and Deci's self-determination theory examines these and recognizes that the most important factor of motivation is whether or not the person is in charge of choosing their own goals and the reasons those goals are important.[2] They identify three types of "self-determined" motivation: intrinsic, integrated, and identified motivation. Each of these types of motivation is influenced by a person's own interests and goals. Intrinsic motivation is the motivation to complete a task for its own value; integrated regulation is feeling motivated by a task while recognizing that there is a benefit to completing it (such as getting a paycheck for a job you like or extra credit in a subject a student enjoys); identified motivation is recognizing that there isn't a lot of motivation for the task itself, however, one values the opportunities it will provide (like working to get good grades in a class because they will lead to opportunities in the future). There are two levels of motivation that are more closely aligned with extrinsic motivation. Introjected regulation is motivation that is derived because of outside social influences, like feeling the need to get good grades because our teachers expect it or "society" tells us it is valued. External regulation is where we fall into bribery, coercion, punishments, sticker charts, and other truly extrinsic factors influencing drive. The final type of motivation Ryan and Deci describe is amotivation – the total lack of motivation that can't be budged, no matter what external rewards or consequences are offered.

You may notice that in previous chapters when we've worked on skill building with kids, I've leaned away from rewards as much as possible. In the steps to build executive functioning skills, for example, you'll notice that the intent of the data collection was not to earn extra money or video game time. It also wasn't to avoid a punishment. (Note: Rewards and punishments are two sides of the same coin. The removal of a reward is perceived as a punishment.) Our kids were the ones who were encouraged to evaluate their own progress.

The problem with rewards is that when a person is working toward earning a reward, their motivation to continue that task declines after the reward is earned. This is true even if the activity was one that the person enjoyed prior to the implementation of the reward. Alfie Kohn's book *Punished by Rewards: The Trouble with Gold Stars, Incentive Plans, A's, Praise, and Other Bribes* explores this phenomenon in detail and applies it to the home, school, and workplace environments.[3] Additionally, many gifted or neurodivergent kids are not motivated by rewards at all. They often see them for what they are: attempts to manipulate them into compliance. Kids and teens who experience demand avoidance are especially suspicious of rewards.

If there comes a time when you feel that some type of a consequence is necessary, natural consequences are the most effective learning tools, meaning that the result of an action is something that automatically follows. For example, if someone doesn't turn in their homework, getting a bad grade is a natural consequence. If, however, the natural consequence isn't meaningful for your child (for example, they don't really care if they fail a class), logical consequences are the next most effective. An example of a logical consequence is that if a child doesn't complete their homework because they've been playing video games, removing the video games until the work is complete is a logical consequence. Additionally, the length of time or intensity of a logical consequence may not have the desired impact on behavior. While a punishment of grounding a child from electronics for two weeks might seem like it will help the child "learn a lesson," that lesson is likely no more effective than a shorter-term logical consequence and a solution-focused conversation.

I understand that there are some times when the only thing that will motivate a kiddo to finish their work by the end of the semester is the threat of losing their phone and that there are times when we'll promise treats or rewards to gain compliance. However, these short-term fixes will undermine your child's motivation in the future. Finding ways to foster authentic motivation through a trusting and safe relationship is not only a more effective and healthy way to support your child, but it also will reinforce your relationship with them.

Case Studies in Motivation: Identified Regulation

I was working with a gifted/autistic high school student who was frustrated with his pre-AP chemistry class.

> All through school, I've been promised that if I do well in my classes, when I get to high school, I'll get to take challenging coursework. But now, when I ask a question to my teacher, they just tell me it is something that will be covered in the next level of chemistry classes. Why should I even bother to answer the teacher's questions when she won't answer mine?

I validated his experience and talked about how I could understand that he didn't feel motivated to complete or turn in his work for a class that was unchallenging. We then talked about the level of motivation, and I asked him to identify where he felt like he was as far as motivation. He identified that he was wavering between introjected motivation and amotivation. We talked about how he *is* intrinsically motivated to learn the concepts and that he is learning them, although at a more rapid pace than his peers. Through our conversation, he was able to realize that he *is* motivated to do well in the class because he wants to go into some type of a science- or math-based career, and doing well in this class is going to give him the opportunities to get into the school he prefers and possibly earn scholarships to attend. This moved him into a self-determined level of motivation – identified regulation – because he was able to identify a specific outcome that was important to him, even if the class itself wasn't motivating.

Case Study in Motivation: Future Orientation

One component that can make finding motivation hard for students is the fact that many neurodivergent kids struggle with long-term future orientation. If executive functioning difficulties are present, awareness of time and the sustainability of long-term goals is difficult. In the previous case study, my client had been aware of his college and career goals since he was young. Another client, who is also gifted/autistic, has a difficult time thinking about the future because it causes significant feelings of overwhelm. Most of his schoolwork is completed based on introjected or external regulation; he doesn't value the learning himself, but he knows he needs to get it done or there will be a consequence at home, like losing video game time. Because he doesn't have any specific long-term goals, it is hard to tie the success of his current coursework to future opportunities. We've been slowly and gradually working to build his ability to consider long-term goals based on what he wants his adult life to look like, what types of things he enjoys, and what is realistic as far as future education. Future options were a topic of conversations over a few years, which generally ended in statements like, "I don't know what I want to do! It gives me too much anxiety to think about!" We recently had a breakthrough when he was able to identify a few possible career paths that seemed like they might be options he could see himself pursuing. This gradual approach to gently addressing the things that motivate him, exploring the aspects of his personality that would influence his success in certain careers, and continued guidance toward building a stronger future orientation is helping him see a successful future for himself. We're now able to work on moving his motivation for the last part of his academic career toward one that is self-determined.

Case Study in Motivation: Learned Helplessness

Identified as gifted in first grade and dyslexic in fourth grade, my client had always been extremely motivated to excel in school. With tutoring and accommodations, she continued to work hard at developing her spelling and reading skills; she was a passionate storyteller and wanted to be an author or a movie director when she grew up. By middle school, she opted not to take the honors courses available because she was worried about keeping up; however, the general education classes were unchallenging on a cognitive level. In order to escape the boredom of the classrooms, she would request to go to the resource teacher who was available to help her with any reading or writing tasks that were assigned. Slowly, she stopped pushing herself. Her goal of being an author or movie director became a far-fetched idea because, as she described it, "There's going to be way too much reading and writing in those classes." Without that finish line waiting for her, her motivation waned. She gradually became more dependent on reinforcement and help from others, unwilling to take risks or attempt challenging tasks. The effort to support her without the balance of challenging opportunities led to a sense of learned helplessness and lack of motivation. During our counseling sessions, we worked to identify ways for her to find things that were motivating for her. She showed a glimmer of interest in participating in theatre in high school and finally got up the confidence to audition. Students in the theatre program were given the opportunity to write and direct their own one-act and she found that spark of motivation. Her efforts paid off, and her one-act was chosen to be showcased at the school. The success stoked her motivation, and filtered through to her academic risk-taking, too.

Case Study in Motivation: Motivation without a Motive

A sophomore in high school, my client was a straight-A student. She was taking all of the AP courses available to her and was ranked number one in her class. She had always been a highly motivated student, but she was carrying a level of stress with her that was unhealthy. She felt she had painted herself in a corner, and despite the anxiety and depression she was experiencing, she didn't feel she could escape. While choosing courses for the following year, she wanted to continue to take as many advanced courses as possible, despite the anguish her course load was causing. Processing her decision-making, she recognized the disconnect. She didn't really *care* about the classes or what she was learning; it was the grades that she identified as important.

Succeeding in school was the goal and without any purpose beyond that, she felt frustrated and stuck. Her motivation beyond academics, however, was low. She didn't have any drive to get a job, and although she wanted friends, any of the possible ways to get to know new people, like joining school clubs, were uninteresting to her. Looking forward to possible college pathways is terrifying because she has no idea what career field she wants to enter. Recently, she completed a job application and recognizes that finding a job might help her find some balance in her life. We're still searching for the purpose for her motivation.

Using the PATHS Process

We all want to help our children find and channel their motivation in a way that is authentic based on their personality and important based on their values. As parents, we are the first navigators of our children's goals and progress. We can help transition to responsibility for that motivation through ongoing conversations designed to build your child's awareness of their goals. The PATHS Process conversation is based on the psychological intervention of motivational interviewing, which has been shown to improve long-term effects for a variety of health- and behavior-related topics when implemented by professionals and parents.[4]

I created the framework of the PATHS Process to structure conversations to help kids identify and narrow their goals, solidify their motives for those goals, and create a framework for reaching them. Additionally, because the child is the driver of this process, we are establishing a framework for motivation that is self-determined and falls into the identified or integrated regulation categories, even if the motivation is not fully intrinsic. The PATHS Process involves five steps:

P – Purpose
A – Awareness
T – Task
H – Hurdles & Helpers
S – Successes.

The PATHS Process can be simple or complex. It might be a five- or ten-minute conversation you have on a car ride. Or it might be an opportunity to have a more structured and lengthy conversation with your child. At the end of this chapter, there is an outline you can use with your child to help navigate this conversation. Using this structured format may be beneficial if you child benefits from concrete and tangible plans; it might also be useful to develop the routine of a PATHS Process conversation, which can be revisited as your child matures. The PATHS Process is also a strategy that is useful for twice-exceptional children who experience demand avoidance because it is driven by the child and their level of comfort.

P – Purpose

Start the conversation with your child about exploring why motivation is important in this particular situation. What is their ultimate purpose that they are motivated to achieve? This is often a bigger picture or longer-term goal. For example, their purpose might be tied to college and career opportunities, like being accepted to a certain school, pursuing a particular topic of study, or earning college scholarships. Their purpose may be something more ambiguous and existential, like helping to reduce homelessness or caring for the environment. It could also be something very concrete and timely, like being able to make new friends, having more time for video games, or making a competitive sports team.

Some kids might be able to easily identify their purpose or big picture goal. Others might have a harder time. Some questions to guide this part of the conversation include:

♦ What are the things that are important to you?
♦ How do you like to spend your time?
♦ What would make your life better?

The final question in the Purpose section of the PATHS Process conversation is a two-part question. Daniel Pink originally framed this question in his book, *Drive: The Surprising Truth about What Motivates Us.*[5] We want to ask our children how *ready for change* they are on a scale of 1 to 10. The follow-up question to ask is *why didn't they choose a lower number?* The answer they give us for why they didn't choose a lower number is the baseline for their motivation. What are the things that are really pushing them to want to change?

A – Awareness

The typical advice that people give to help motivate kids might be applicable and useful in the most vague and generalizable ways, but to actually find strategies and tools that will foster success, effort, and motivation, our twice-exceptional kids need something more. The basis for this "more" is an awareness of self. Understanding our own strengths and struggles is empowering because even though it might feel uncomfortable to recognize or think about our difficulties, it isn't helpful to bury our heads in the sand and pretend they don't exist. Just like the accommodations our kids need at school, we need to encourage them to set goals and take steps that are a fit for their current level of ability. This is a type of self-scaffolding; helping kids challenge themselves just enough.

Awareness of self is much broader than the strengths and struggles related to academics. Some other areas your child should consider include:

♦ Hobbies or other areas of interest
♦ Relationships with other people
♦ Self-confidence in unfamiliar situations
♦ Risk-taking or risk-aversion
♦ Attention to detail within specified domains.

A solid self-awareness will help your child develop a sense of realistic optimism that they are working toward a goal that is manageable. It will also boost their willingness to try new strategies if they feel their purpose is aligned with their personality. There are many kids who perceive the world around them and absorb the expectations they see put forth by society. Self-awareness gives kids the confidence to shed those expectations and channel their motivation through their authentic selves. I think we can all relate to the experience of trying to be something we're not. Twice-exceptional kids are frequently put in the position of trying to be something they're not. There are few things that will zap a person's motivation more quickly than being forced to try to fit a personality or experience that isn't genuine.

T – Task

The next step in the PATHS Process is to help our kids integrate their purpose and awareness of self into the specific task or goal they find personally valuable. The task portion of this process should create a concrete goal they would like to achieve, which will move them one step closer to their purpose. The ability for this task to be manageable and within reach is vital to foster the success/ motivation virtuous cycle. The task should also have an identified outcome, so your child is able to identify when they complete it.

It may be helpful to brainstorm a list of possible tasks before deciding on one. Each task may correlate to a step that would be necessary toward the larger purpose. Or there may not be a sequential list of tasks that fit for your child's big picture purpose. Either way, having a few options to choose from as a task is helpful. The effort that is used to achieve this task accumulates as progress toward the bigger picture goal defined as purpose. The focus on small, discrete skills and steps helps neurodivergent kids gradually build confidence where they may have felt overwhelmed before. It also helps them develop their own strengths-based strategies to move toward their goals.

You may find that the task your child chooses isn't what you would prioritize as the most important and influential factor in their daily life. While it may feel difficult to give your child the latitude they desire in setting these goals, remember that self-efficacy will generalize to other areas of their life. Twice-exceptional kids who've felt unsuccessful because their neurodivergence doesn't fit the typical mold need to have successes that are meaningful to them. Empowering them to take risks and move toward goals they see as important is never time that is wasted.

H – Hurdles & Helpers

A straightforward and clear analysis of the possible hurdles that may inhibit your child's ability to manage these tasks is necessary. Proactive planning is an important skill for your child and is a useful skill to use when working to self-advocate in a variety of settings. Drawing from the exploration of strengths and struggles completed during the awareness step of the PATHS Process and considering the specific components of the identified task, identify as many obstacles as possible that may inhibit your child's success. Where might they need help? What supports might they need? What might prevent them from being able to accomplish their task? From this list of specific hurdles, develop a plan of action to overcome the hurdles. This might be a something that can occur prior to your child beginning to work on the task or it might be several options that could be determined based on what they need through the process.

Take the time to scaffold the support that your child needs because this is an essential component to their success. Give them the opportunity to identify the areas of difficulty and determine the strategies that will work best for them. This provides autonomy and opportunities for self-advocacy. If your child has an idea or suggestion that is mostly reasonable, try to implement it. Ownership for this process should belong to your child as much as possible; we are there as co-pilot, but they are in charge.

S – Successes

Finally, celebrate the successes with your child. Gifted kids are notorious for forgetting the gradual progress that is generally necessary to reach any goal. Additionally, to achieve the purpose they defined at the outset of the PATHS Process, there are going to be a range of steps that need to be implemented. Don't let the gradual progress deter your child. Whether you keep a list of the tasks that have been attempted and achieved or you bring them up during conversations as a gentle reminder of the successes they've already had, keeping the successes in mind fosters a willingness to continue to work toward the goal. Even if your child *wasn't* successful at achieving the task they set out to reach, reframing the disappointment as an opportunity to readjust expectations and refine the strategies they were using or as an opportunity to add more information to what is known about what works or doesn't work for your child is helpful.

Use this outline as a format to guide a discussion about motivation and goal setting. Jot some notes down about each question in the column on the right to help with decision-making or to revisit your thoughts in the future.

PATHS Process discussion outline

P **Purpose**
What is important to you?

How do you like to spend your
time?

What goals do you have for the
future (long- or short-term)?

What would make your life
better?

On a scale of 1 to 10, how ready
are you to start on your task?

Follow-up question: Why didn't
you pick a lower number?

A **Assessment**
How would you describe your
personality?

What strengths do you have that
have helped you?

What are some successes you've
had in the past? Struggles?

How do you best learn?

How do you connect with other
people?

T Task

What are some specific tasks that you could put into action right away would help you move toward your purpose?

How do the tasks you've listed implement your strengths?

Choose one task that you would like to implement.

How will you know when the task is complete?

H Hurdles & Helpers

What possible obstacles might prevent you from completing your task?

Are there certain supports that might help?

Whose help do you need?

S Successes

Reflecting on the effort to complete your task, what worked and what didn't? Did you complete your task?

How did working on this task influence your progress toward your purpose?

Even if you were unable to complete your task, what did you learn?

What is the next step that will continue to help you achieve your purpose?

Sample PATHS Process discussion outlines

P   Purpose

What is important to you?	*My friends, playing piano and drums*
How do you like to spend your time?	*Doing jazz band at school, playing video games with my friends, riding my bike*
What goals do you have for the future (long- or short-term)?	*Starting a band with my friends, going to college, passing my classes*
What would make your life better?	*Less homework! Better grades, no missing work.*
On a scale of 1 to 10, how ready are you to start working toward your goal? *Follow-up question*: Why didn't you pick a lower number?	*On a scale of 1 to 10, I'm at a 6.5. I didn't pick a lower number because I know that the things I really want to do are all based on being able to do some of these things.*

A   Assessment

How would you describe your personality?	*Friendly, silly, a little disorganized, stressed out when there is too much to do*
What strengths do you have that have helped you?	*I learn fast and do well on my tests. I am good at playing music and that makes me less stressed.*
What are some successes you've had in the past? Struggles?	*Got into jazz band, have gotten pretty good grades. Can't get my work done in class anymore and I hate homework.*
How do you best learn?	*Listening to my teachers and doing work in school. Watching videos on YouTube to explain things.*
How do you connect with other people?	*Texting, talking at lunch, playing online video games*

T   Task

What are some specific tasks that you could put into action right away would help you move toward your purpose?	*Ask a couple friends about starting a band*
	Find time to get schoolwork done – maybe asking to move my study hall earlier in the day or staying after school to do work at library so I don't have homework

How do the tasks you've listed implement your strengths?	*Starting a band uses my ability to connect with my friends and my musical abilities*
	Finding alternatives for schoolwork allows me to do well in school and earn grades that reflect my ability
Choose one task that you would like to implement.	*I really want to start a band with my friends!*
How will you know when the task is complete?	*I'll know the task is complete when I have a couple other friends who want to do the band with me and we've had a few practices together.*

H   Hurdles & Helpers

What possible obstacles might prevent you from completing your task?	*Other people may not want to do this with me*
	People might not have time
	I might be stressed trying to manage school and an extra band practice
Are there certain supports that might help?	*Starting a group chat with the people who want to be in the band*
	Making a list of possible practice spaces and getting permission to practice there
Whose help do you need?	*Bandmates, parents (for permission to practice and maybe transportation)*

S   Successes

Reflecting on the effort to complete your task, what worked and what didn't? Did you complete your task?	*We were able to get people to agree to be in the band and YES we completed the task of having a few practices. The hardest part was trying to figure out what music to play.*
How did working on this task influence your progress toward your purpose?	*It made me realize that there might be something I really can do in music when I go to college because it is the thing I really love.*
Even if you were unable to complete your task, what did you learn?	*We completed the task, but we are still having a hard time finding practice time that works for everyone.*

What is the next step that will continue to help you achieve your purpose?	*We're going to keep having practices. I'm going to make sure I manage my grades so I can keep doing competitive jazz band in school.*

P   Purpose

What is important to you?	*My family, my pets, doing LEGO robotics competitions*
How do you like to spend your time?	*Building with LEGOs, watching movies, playing games with my family, reading*
What goals do you have for the future (long- or short-term)?	*I want to make more friends so I have someone to play with at recess at school. I want to create video games and apps for my career.*
What would make your life better?	*More friends*
On a scale of 1 to 10, how ready are you to start on your task?	*I'm at a 5. I didn't pick a lower number because I get really lonely at recess and want some friends to play with.*
Follow-up question: Why didn't you pick a lower number?	

A   Assessment

How would you describe your personality?	*Nice. I take care of my pets a lot. I don't like a lot of noise or when kids in class are too wound up. I like to learn a lot.*
What strengths do you have that have helped you?	*I am inventive and can figure stuff out. I am good at drawing.*
What are some successes you've had in the past? Struggles?	*We got 1st place at our LEGO robotics competition. Nobody at school really wants to play with me.*
How do you best learn?	*I can learn by trying things and figuring them out. I don't like to do too many worksheets because they are boring.*
How do you connect with other people?	*Doing stuff together. I get nervous about talking to people sometimes and I don't always like to do the same stuff the other kids like during recess.*

T   Task

What are some specific tasks that you could put into action right away would help you move toward your purpose?	*Learn more about robotics* *Learn more about coding* *Get some more friends*

How do the tasks you've listed implement your strengths?	*I like technology.*
Choose one task that you would like to implement.	*Get to know one or two kids who I can play with at recess.*
How will you know when the task is complete?	*If I have someone to talk to and play with during recess.*

H Hurdles & Helpers

What possible obstacles might prevent you from completing your task?	*Kids don't want to do what I like – they always just want to play sports. I get nervous about talking to the other kids that I don't know very much.*
Are there certain supports that might help?	*I might try to plan out something to say before I talk to people.*
Whose help do you need?	*Maybe the school counselor or my teacher?*

S Successes

Reflecting on the effort to complete your task, what worked and what didn't? Did you complete your task?	*I was too nervous to start talking to anyone, but the school counselor helped me get to know a new student at school who also wanted to get to know some people. Yes! Because we hang out during lunch and recess. He might join the LEGO robotics team, too.*
How did working on this task influence your progress toward your purpose?	*Helped me feel better and not so lonely during school.*
Even if you were unable to complete your task, what did you learn?	
What is the next step that will continue to help you achieve your purpose?	*I want to invite my friend over to the house on a weekend sometime.*

Chapter Reflection

- ◆ What are some goals you have for your child? What goals do they have for themselves? Do these align?
- ◆ What types of motivation/regulation can you identify in your own life? What about when you were a child? (Refer to the section on self-determination theory for a description of each.)
- ◆ How would you describe your relationship with your child? Do you feel that you are constantly pushing your child? Are there areas where you can allow them more autonomy?

Notes

1. Ridgley, L. M., DaVia Rubenstein, L., & Callan, G. L. (2020). Gifted underachievement within a self-regulated learning framework: Proposing a task-dependent model to guide early identification and intervention. *Psychology in the Schools, 57*(9), 1365–1384. doi:10.1002/pits.22408
2. Ryan, R. M., & Deci, E. L. (2018). *Self-determination theory: Basic psychological needs in motivation, development, and wellness*. New York: Guilford Press.
3. Kohn, A. (2018). *Punished by rewards: The trouble with gold stars, incentive plans, A's, praise, and other bribes*. Boston: Mariner Books/ Houghton Mifflin Harcourt.
4. Mutschler, C., Naccarato, E., Rouse, J., Davey, C., & McShane, K. (2018). Realist-informed review of motivational interviewing for adolescent health behaviors. *Systematic Reviews, 7*(1). doi:10.1186/ s13643–018–0767–9
5. Pink, D. H. (2011). *Drive: The surprising truth about what motivates us*. New York: Riverhead Books.

PART
IV

Finding the Right Academic Fit

Finding the right academic fit for your child can be a challenge. Navigating the school system to advocate for the services your child needs and deserves can be daunting. Twice-exceptional kids are often in schools that don't understand (or *won't* understand) their unique needs. This section of the book will help you figure out how to make the most of your child's educational placement, whether you are advocating for gifted education classes, special education services, or accommodations in their general classroom.

As a former teacher and school counselor in public schools, I genuinely believe that educators want to do what is best for every kid. The systemic issues that arise due to funding constraints are difficult to escape. Even in private school settings, services may not be available for kids with unique needs in the school setting. And try as you might to find the perfect school for your child, I've often found the success of a student is directly tied to their relationship with their individual teacher. It can be in the best school in the state, but if your child has a teacher that doesn't "click" with them, it is going to be a rough school year. They might be in a school that doesn't have the highest ratings, but an understanding teacher, counselor, or administrator can make all the difference in your child's success.

DOI: 10.4324/9781003237532-16

My hope is that you will find ways to effectively collaborate with the school to advocate for your child and that the school will be receptive to understanding your child's needs. This section will cover ideas about how to communicate with the school, possible types of school placements you may want to consider for your twice-exceptional child, and information about how to access the appropriate types of services for your child.

12

Assessing Educational Options

The complexity of twice-exceptional children makes finding an appropriate academic setting for them difficult. As a parent, how can you seek out the best options for your child? If you have few options, how can you make the most of what is available? 2e kids can thrive in many environments, but each has its own pros and cons. Navigating the educational world and finding the best fit can be overwhelming, but knowing what types of questions to ask is helpful.

Types of Educational Settings

Public Schools

A majority of students attend public schools and the opportunities available within those schools vary greatly depending on state mandates concerning funding and decisions made by your local school board. While some public schools have a reputation for being underperforming, they often offer the most flexibility and options for twice-exceptional kids.

Some benefits to public schools include the fact that public schools often have the resources to offer services to kids with unique learning needs. For example, they generally have speech–language services, special education services, or gifted

DOI: 10.4324/9781003237532-17

services available on-site. Flexibility for accommodations can be greater in a public-school setting, partially because they serve many children with diverse needs and are more accustomed to being flexible with how they support kids in the classroom. Tools and technology to accommodate twice-exceptional learners may be available because the schools are prepared to serve students with a variety of needs. A drawback for public schools is that qualifying for services or programs may be difficult for twice-exceptional students based on criteria that are established at the district or state level, often because a child isn't "struggling enough" to qualify for services.

Magnet Schools

Magnet schools are also a type of public school controlled by the local school district. Magnet schools frequently offer specialized programs, which might be a great option for twice-exceptional kids' diverse learning profiles. Attending a school that specializes in math and science might be perfect for your math-y kid. Other magnet schools might focus on performing arts or humanities. Because these schools are public, they are free to attend, however, they often require both an application with assessment information, and gaining admission can be competitive. While Section 504 plans and IEPs are available, various magnet schools can vary greatly in their ability to provide specific services. Teachers who aren't commonly used to supporting twice-exceptional students may be unfamiliar with providing accommodations for advanced coursework; additionally, staffing for specialized services can vary if a school has only a small number of students who require a specific type of educational support.

Charter Schools

Charter schools are available in some states or metropolitan areas. Charter schools are publicly funded (aka: free) but are run by groups outside the local school districts. While charter schools must allow all children to attend their programs, some charters that are in high demand may use a lottery system to limit the number of students based on the space available in the school. By law, charter schools are required to offer the opportunity to enroll to all students who wish to attend and are not allowed to require admissions testing. This means that charter schools are required to provide supports for children with IEPs or Section 504 plans. However, other factors may influence whether it would be a good fit for your child. For example, charter schools have a lot of latitude in the style of programs they provide. If you are considering a charter school, examine how the school discusses students who need accommodations and the type of educational model they follow. Do they differentiate within the classroom or offer small group and individualized support for struggling learners? How do they handle discipline issues? How big are their class sizes? Charter schools shouldn't be ruled out for twice-exceptional kids, but parents should thoroughly investigate the schools before applying.

Vocational High School Programs

For some of our twice-exceptional learners, the opportunity to attend a vocational high school program can be a lifeline to thrive in high school. In the past, programs like these were viewed as the option for students who weren't college-bound, but the structure of many programs now provides an opportunity for a student to learn a trade and then pursue it further upon graduation, if they choose. For our twice-exceptional students who love hands-on learning or have a talent in an area such as computer technology or mechanical repair, a vocational program that allows them to pursue an area of interest while earning their high school diploma *plus* additional trainings or certifications. Twice-exceptional students who don't have an IEP or Section 504 plan may not be made aware of vocational programs through the schools, so parents should consider looking into what types of programs are available to students and how to apply if they believe it may be a good option for their child. Additional types of programs offered range from the fields of hospitality, medicine, childcare, and more. Some programs last all four years of high school and others are only available for students in their junior and senior years. They generally require some type of application process, so considering options at least one or two semesters ahead of when your child would be interested in enrolling is necessary.

Virtual Schools

Now that the pandemic has normalized the existence of virtual schools, many students may find themselves with the option to continue to attend classes online. Virtual school provides an excellent option for students who are good candidates for subject acceleration (for example, taking math classes that are one or more years beyond their grade level) because coordinating the logistics of this type of acceleration can make it difficult to provide coursework to students if they are the only student in a building who is ready to take a certain course. Another unexpected benefit of virtual schooling for some twice-exceptional students was the removal of the stresses of daily social interactions and rapid pacing of transitions throughout the school day. Of course, virtual school for many kids isn't a good option because the structure of the classroom along with in-person instruction provides more support, and the implementation of IEPs and Section 504 plans is complicated when instructing virtually.

Private Schools

Private schools can be a good option for some twice-exceptional learners, but the many variables make it necessary to consider this on a case-by-case basis. Some private schools offer rigorous instruction to challenge and engage high-ability learners; others are set up to provide support for the social and emotional needs of neurodivergent students. Some private schools are extremely flexible in how they support neurodivergent kids, while others have a difficult time making even basic accommodations. Unless a school specifically caters to the needs of neurodivergent kids, many private schools are unprepared to offer the types of accommodations and supports that might be most helpful for your child. Private school teachers may have had limited training in the needs of neurodivergent students and have little, if any, support or resources at the school to access. Some private schools may offer additional supports, but only at an added expense for families. If you are considering a private school, ask specific questions about the strategies they use to support 2e children, such as the types of accommodations they frequently use and how they address discipline. If you are able to afford a private school, if you can find one that specializes in the type of learner your child is, you will benefit.

Home schools

Many families of twice-exceptional kids opt for the freedom of homeschooling because they find more traditional schools are not able to support their children effectively. Homeschooling provides the flexibility for you and your child to collaboratively determine the style and pace of instruction that are best. Homeschooling families are generally resourceful, finding a combination of curricula created specifically for homeschooling families, online programs, and in-person co-ops (a group of homeschooling families who collaborate for some topics). Some families find university-model private schools, which are a hybrid of in-person learning two or three days per week and independent work at home the other days of the week. State laws vary with how homeschooling must be registered or documented, so if you are considering this option for your family, be sure to check into the regulations in your state. Some families are unable to homeschool, due to parental work obligations. Other parents feel they aren't able to effectively homeschool their neurodivergent child because they worry that they can't appropriately support their child or recognize from a self-care standpoint that educating their children at home isn't best.

Gifted Education Services

If your child hasn't already been identified as gifted, but you suspect their ability warrants gifted education services, your school may allow you to request for them to be assessed for gifted education services. However, often a single score on a cognitive ability test isn't all that is needed to access gifted education services. Understanding how the school your child attends serves students with advanced cognitive ability and the types of options available can help you determine the best way to advocate for your child.

The field of gifted education has been under fire recently for difficulties with inequity in gifted programming across the nation. White and Asian-American students tend to be over-represented in many gifted programs, while Black, Latino, and other culturally diverse groups are under-represented.[1] This reckoning of difficult facts has led to a necessary reevaluation of how students are identified for gifted education services and what those services should look like in the schools.

This means different things for families of twice-exceptional children, depending on where you live and how your district is managing these changes. Some districts are adopting alternative identification plans for traditionally under-represented groups, which sometimes can include expanded methods for identifying twice-exceptional students. This can help more 2e kids access gifted education services. Other districts are creating big shifts in how they provide opportunities for their bright students and closely aligning their services with specific talent development in content areas. This can work for or against 2e learners, depending on where a child's specific skills are. Other schools are moving to using "local norms" to identify students for advanced learning opportunities. This means that instead of using the benchmarks created by the national averages on cognitive and academic tests, schools are looking specifically at their local student populations and providing gifted or advanced learning opportunities to the top performers in their school or district.

Because the benchmark for accessing gifted services is dependent on the school district where you live, your child may be "gifted" in one district and, if you move several miles away, no longer eligible for gifted services in a different district. Does your child no longer need access to challenging curriculum and a pace that is appropriate for their learning needs? The answer is complicated.

Because parents of 2e kids are often fighting an uphill battle with schools to access services (both gifted and special education), it is helpful to understand the boundaries the schools your school has to work within. For example, some states have funding tied to gifted education services, and if there is money involved, there are likely regulations about where that money goes. Schools may be limited if the state requires that funding is only allowed to support services for students who achieve a specific score on a nationally normed test of cognitive ability or academic achievement. It may be necessary for some schools to use funding to support a specific percentage of a school's student body (for example, the top 2–3% of a student body); in schools where many students are very bright, this means some students whose scores fall in the "gifted" range on IQ tests may still not rank highly enough for gifted services in their schools. Other schools use local norms, which is useful for schools that perform more poorly when compared to national averages. Other states don't recognize giftedness at all, leading public schools to offer little to no support for high-ability learners, at least until options at the middle and high school levels are offered for challenge, honors, or Advanced Placement (AP) courses for students who need more challenging coursework.

Some questions to consider as you are exploring the options for advanced learning opportunities for your child:

- How do students qualify for the program?
- What is the process for referral and assessment? Does the district use universal screening methods (every student in certain grade levels is screened), teacher and parent referrals, or another method to find students?
- Is the program content-based (academic subjects, like reading and math) or enrichment-based (like critical thinking and creativity)?
- What types of accommodations do children with the same type of twice-exceptionality receive in the gifted program?
- If your child also receives special education services, how do those programs cooperate to support students?
- How often does the gifted program meet? For how long does it meet?
- Will my child miss classroom instruction time if they attend the gifted program? (Follow-up: If they

miss classroom instruction, what is the expectation for making up classwork?)

♦ What options are available for students if they don't qualify for gifted education services?

Difficult Decisions

It is important for parents and their twice-exceptional children to strongly consider the benefits and drawbacks to various styles of advanced learner programs. The kneejerk response to whether or not a gifted child should receive gifted education services is, "Of course!" However, on an individual level, there is more to this decision than meets the eye. Different programs provide different types of supports, and there may be times that a student would benefit from opting out of certain styles of programs.

For example, let's say a twice-exceptional gifted/dyslexic child qualifies for gifted education services based on their cognitive ability score. They are highly creative and love visual arts. However, the program is a highly language-based program, requiring intense reading and writing. The first step to support this student would be put on the school through requesting accommodations for the student: books on tape, an exemption from spelling counting as a grade for work, etc. But, let's say even with accommodations, this child is feeling stressed out. They are beginning to experience negative feelings about themselves when compared to their peers in the gifted education classroom. Dropping the program may be an acceptable option.

There are times when a district's identification process doesn't closely align with the type of program they provide. I've seen programs that admit students to the gifted program if they score above the 95th percentile on either an academic test or a creativity inventory. The kids who qualified for the program based on the creativity inventory were at a disadvantage because the program was highly academic. Some schools put all of their gifted students into a single Language Arts class to provide their gifted services, whether the child is advanced in Language Arts or not. Does this mean the child who doesn't fit in these programs isn't gifted? Not at all. What it means is that a child would be much better served by a program directly aligned with the skills assessed to qualify them.

If a program isn't a good fit for your child and the benefits don't outweigh the drawbacks, don't feel obligated to keep them there. You have permission to opt out of gifted education services that aren't a fit for your child. Start by advocating for accommodations and asking for support. But also recognize that there are times that a school's identification process doesn't align perfectly with their programming, or times when a gifted program's rapid pace and rigor aren't worth the cost to the emotional wellbeing of a twice-exceptional student. Many schools allow students to take a semester or a year off from participating in their gifted programs and then reenter without requiring new testing, so that may be an option if what the program is currently offering isn't a good fit for where your child is right now.

Acceleration

Acceleration is a term that refers to moving a student through the curriculum at a pace that is faster than their same-age peers. Although there are other types of acceleration, most often this term is used to describe some type of grade skipping. The most familiar form of grade skipping is whole-grade acceleration where a student either completes a grade and is promoted two grade levels or moves mid-year from one grade level to the next. Another option for acceleration is subject-level acceleration. Subject-level acceleration occurs when a student is ready for advanced content in a specific subject area, like math, and attends more advanced instruction in that area while continuing to participate in their same grade for the other subjects. Early entry to kindergarten is another form of acceleration, which is equivalent to whole-grade skipping from preschool to kindergarten.

It is common for people to believe that acceleration is unhealthy for a child's social and emotional development, however, research shows this isn't true. Even for twice-exceptional kids, acceleration can be a good option.[2] In many cases, having the opportunity to participate in instruction that is at a child's cognitive level is actually helpful for their self-esteem because they feel fulfilled and challenged by their schoolwork.

Different schools handle acceleration differently. If you think acceleration of some type might be useful for your child, look into district policies and determine if there is a procedure already in place for requesting acceleration. If your school doesn't have a procedure in place, there are some great tools, such as the Iowa Acceleration Scale, that provide a framework for parents and educators to examine whether a student might be a good candidate for acceleration.

Individualized Education Plans and Section 504 Plans

Twice-exceptional kids may be eligible for support in schools through two different avenues. An Individualized Education Plan (IEP) is a document that provides a student with some type of special education services, meaning that they receive instruction from a special educator to support their needs. The alternate method for providing supports for a student is through a Section 504 plan, which is a document that is based on a medical or psychological diagnosis made outside of the school that outlines the specific accommodations and modifications a student needs in order to adequately access the curriculum. A Section 504 plan does not require the student to receive any additional educational services provided by the school.

Differences between IEPs and Section 504 Plans

The main difference in qualifying for an IEP versus a Section 504 plan is based on whether a child has an educational diagnosis or a medical diagnosis. An educational diagnosis is made by school personnel following an evaluation completed by the school. The categories that can qualify a child for an IEP are designated through the Individuals with Disabilities Education Act (IDEA) and regulated at the federal level by the Office of Special Education in the US Department of Education. If a child doesn't fall under one of these diagnoses, they are unable to access special education services (although they may still be eligible for a Section 504 plan based on a medical diagnosis). The categories that can designate a student eligible to receive special education services are:

- ◆ Autism (differences between educational identification and medical diagnosis vary, impacting twice-exceptional learners; see Qualifying for Special Education Services for Autism, pg. 219)
- ◆ Deaf-blindness
- ◆ Deafness
- ◆ Emotional disturbance (various mental health issues that impact a student's ability to access the curriculum; could include diagnoses related to anxiety, depression, bipolar, OCD, or autism)
- ◆ Hearing impairment (hearing loss not covered by the definition of deafness)
- ◆ Intellectual disability
- ◆ Multiple disabilities (when a child has multiple conditions covered by IDEA)
- ◆ Orthopedic impairment (functioning difficulties related to a student's body; for example, cerebral palsy)
- ◆ Other health impairment (addresses conditions that impact a child's strength, energy, and alertness; includes ADHD)
- ◆ Specific learning disability (includes dyslexia, dyscalculia, dysgraphia, auditory processing disorder, non-verbal learning disorder, etc.)
- ◆ Speech or language impairment (includes speech production difficulty, like pronouncing certain sounds or stuttering)
- ◆ Traumatic brain injury
- ◆ Visual impairment, including blindness.

Eligibility for a Section 504 plan is based on a medical diagnosis made by a medical professional. When we're discussing twice-exceptional kids, these diagnoses generally come through a primary care doctor, neurologist, psychologist, or other mental health professional. (A Section 504 plan can also be implemented for any medical reason, such as a diabetic student needing accommodations to monitor and care for their blood sugar.)

Many twice-exceptional students don't qualify for (and don't need) an IEP but can be supported in the school through a well-developed and -supported Section 504 plan. Section 504 plans are based on how significantly impacted a child's abilities are impacted by their medical diagnosis. The Office of Civil Rights within the US Department of Education specifies that a student's diagnosis must substantially impact a major life activity. Some of the types of life activities that may be impacted for twice-exceptional learners can include:

◆ Performing manual tasks (for example, a student with sensory or processing difficulties may struggle writing by hand or typing)
◆ Thinking (for example, a student with obsessive-compulsive thoughts may need accommodations for difficulties with managing intrusive thoughts during tests and assessments)
◆ Concentrating (for example, an ADHD student who needs support to manage time and focus during class)
◆ Communicating (for example, an autistic student may struggle with effective communication or self-advocacy).

There is not an exclusive list of major life activities that can be included in a Section 504 plan, so other areas can also be considered for accommodations.

The other main difference between an IEP and a Section 504 plan is the way the supports are provided. An IEP guarantees a student specific special education services, which involve the support of a special education teacher. This might mean a student goes to a special education teacher for support in certain subject areas or they are placed in a class that is co-taught by a special education teacher. This teacher may modify the curriculum (specifically adjusting the exact skills that are taught) based on a child's needs. A Section 504 plan is only used to put into place specific accommodations that allow the student to use the same curriculum that other students use and typically does not require instruction from a teacher other than the student's primary classroom teachers.

Qualifying for Special Education Services

If you suspect that your child needs more than just accommodations and modifications for academic success, you can request the school convene a meeting to determine whether there is enough information to complete an assessment for an IEP. The initial meeting is called a Review of Existing Data meeting and is required to take place within 30 days of when the request is made. Parents are included in this meeting, which also includes various members of the school stuff, such as the child's classroom teacher, the counselor, a special education teacher, a school psychologist or psychological examiner, and an administrator. During this meeting, the group (usually referred to as a "team") looks at data from classwork, assessments, observations, and standardized tests to determine if they feel there is the possibility that a disability is present and whether it is valuable to complete testing to determine whether a child might qualify for special education services.

Many parents of twice-exceptional children have a difficult time getting over this first barrier to accessing special education services because their 2e child might look like they are "doing okay" academically based on the work they are completing in the classroom and their achievement on various tests. If a child has already been identified for the gifted program, parents may be able to refer back to those test scores and point out that a child's ability should generally approach their cognitive skills and, if a child is at or just below grade level expectations, that can be a sign that there is something else (such as a learning disability) that is holding the child back.

If the school agrees that there is more information that would be useful to determine the presence of a disability, the team identifies the specific areas to assess (for example, cognitive ability, academic skills, or social/emotional functioning) and, with parent permission, moves forward with testing. Once testing is complete, the team reconvenes and goes over the results of the assessment. They talk through each of the possible areas of disability established by IDEA and determine whether or not the student qualifies for services.

Qualifying for Special Education Services for Specific Learning Disabilities

When assessing a bright child for support in reading, writing, or math, schools tend to rely on the ability–achievement discrepancy model to identify a "specific learning disability" (SLD). This is a difficult hurdle to clear when securing academic special education services for twice-exceptional children because schools often rely on two measures to qualify a student for services based on the ability–achievement discrepancy model. First, they look for a "significant discrepancy" between a child's ability and achievement – usually a benchmark of 22.5+ points of difference between a student's ability (IQ) and academic achievement scores. The second criterion looks for the achievement scores to be below average; assuming that a twice-exceptional child's cognitive ability falls at about the 95th percentile or higher (>124) and expecting their academic achievement scores to be in the below average range of the 10th percentile or lower (<80), we're looking for a difference in scores of 45 or more points! Some schools, like Montgomery County Schools in Maryland, established alternate score benchmarks for high-ability children to qualify for support based on their IQ. A student with an IQ score of 130–139 can qualify for services with achievement scores less than or equal to 100; a student with an IQ score between 120–129 can qualify for services with achievement scores less than or equal to 94.[3]

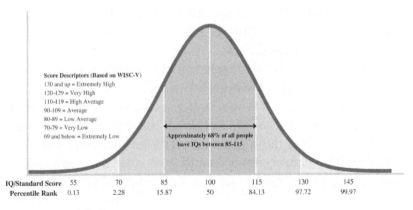

FIGURE 12.1 IQ bell curve

This leeway gives bright kids a pathway to the support they need, without needing to meet the benchmark of scores that are considered "below average" for the general population of students.

Qualifying for Special Education Services through a Medical Diagnosis

Although typically a medical diagnosis will lead to eligibility for a Section 504 plan, there are occasions when a child may be able to access special education services due to a medical diagnosis. The educational diagnosis "other health impaired" (OHI) can provide some leeway for school districts to provide services for students who may not meet other eligibility criteria. For example, a student with ADHD might be assessed due to concerns in academics, but not meet the requirements based on the ability–achievement discrepancy. If it appears, however, that the ADHD is impacting their overall achievement because they are unable to focus or have poor working memory, considering an OHI diagnosis may allow them to access services through special education.

Qualifying for Special Education Services for Autism

The requirements set forth for students to receive a diagnosis and services under IDEA for autism are different than the criteria used to identify autism in the medical community. Twice-exceptional gifted/autistic kids may be unable to qualify for special education based on a diagnosis of educational autism (even if they have a medical diagnosis of autism) because of the way the diagnosis is defined in IDEA and variability between states.[4] The definition provided for educational autism states:

> Autism means a developmental disability significantly affecting verbal and nonverbal communication and social interaction, generally evident before age three, that adversely affects a child's educational performance. Other characteristics often associated with autism are engagement in repetitive activities and stereotyped movements, resistance to environmental change or change in daily routines, and unusual responses to sensory experience.

Autism does not apply if a child's educational performance is adversely affected primarily because the child has an emotional disturbance.

While some 2e students may qualify for services to support areas such as pragmatic (social) language, many twice-exceptional gifted/autistic students mask and compensate for communication- and social interaction-based difficulties through their advanced cognitive abilities. This means some schools may opt to identify a student with a medical diagnosis of autism under the educational diagnosis of "emotional disturbance."

Qualifying for Special Education Services for Emotional and Behavioral Concerns

For students who show significant struggle with regulating their emotions and behaviors at school, they may qualify for an IEP based on an educational diagnosis of "emotional disturbance" (ED). Some twice-exceptional students with diagnoses of ADHD or autism may find that the only category they qualify for services under is ED because their struggles are related to regulating their emotions as opposed to their academics. Some autistic students need special education services but don't qualify for a diagnosis of educational autism because their language skills don't lag enough for them to qualify for that diagnosis. As a neurodiversity advocate, it bothers me greatly that the only way some neurodivergent students can access support services is through a diagnosis called "emotional disturbance," however, I try to chalk it up to legislators making policy and try to focus on the services a child will receive, instead of the label given.

Creating the Individualized Education Plan

Once the team has agreed that a student is eligible for an IEP, they meet to create the education plan. In addition to identifying the specific types of services the student will receive, the exact number of minutes the student will receive these services each week is set. The education plan also includes specific goals tied to the student's needs. For example, some possible IEP goals for a twice-exceptional student may include:

♦ While reading aloud, Regena will implement knowledge of consonants, consonant blends, and common vowel patterns to decode unfamiliar words with 90% accuracy in 4/5 times.

♦ Given number sentences without an addition (+), subtraction (−), or equals (=) sign, Amir will choose the correct symbol to complete the number sentence with 80% accuracy in three trials.

♦ Elias will correctly write and punctuate a paragraph with dialogue that includes at least 3 exchanges with 80% accuracy in 2/3 trials.

♦ When Sawyer needs to correct another individual, he will look at the person, remain calm, be specific about the behavior, tell why it is a problem, and listen to the other person's explanation on 4/5 conversations with 100% accuracy.

IEP goals are created to be discrete and skill-specific, so the special educator who is responsible for supporting the student can measure the progress and report back to the IEP team at specified reporting periods. The IEP team will meet every year to go over the IEP, assess progress toward goals, and create new goals, if needed. In addition to the specific goals, accommodations and modifications that can be used to support the student are also included in an IEP.

Every three years, the student will be reevaluated for special education services unless you and the team determine it is not necessary. For example, if a student has completed a cognitive ability test previously, the results are likely to be the same, and if the results are unlikely to influence the implementation of the IEP, it may be decided that asking the child to go through this process again is unneeded. If a student has continued to reach their goals and no longer needs the support of the IEP, they can be released from the IEP. Sometimes when a child is released from an IEP, they may qualify for a Section 504 plan to ensure that accommodations and modifications are still made to support the student without the additional support of special education services.

Section 504 Plans

Section 504 plans are frequently created to support twice-exceptional students with medical diagnoses that impact their ability to be successful in the classroom. A Section 504 plan is a document that designates specific accommodations and modifications that can be implemented throughout a student's typical school day. Although they may modify the *way* the student shows mastery of the curriculum, a Section 504 plan does not include changes to the curriculum itself.

Eligibility for a Section 504 plan is determined by the impact of a medical diagnosis on a student's ability to succeed in the typical classroom setting.

Schools may vary in how they identify students for Section 504 plans. In general, the process typically follows a pattern similar to the one outlined here:

1. Child receives a medical diagnosis and is struggling in school. The referral process is started by a parent, counselor, or teacher recommending that the child be considered for accommodations through a Section 504 plan. Documentation from a medical professional to verify the medical diagnosis is typically requested.

2. The team meets to discuss the ways the child is impacted by their diagnosis. They must determine how significantly impacted the child is by their diagnosis. Evidence must show that a student is "substantially impacted" by their diagnosis to qualify for a Section 504 plan.

3. Some schools may complete some assessments or questionnaires to determine the specific areas a child is impacted; other schools may be able to use observational data from the Section 504 team.

    a. It is important that mitigating factors are excluded when determining the impact of a diagnosis on a child's ability to succeed at school without accommodations. For example, taking medication for ADHD is considered a mitigating factor, as are additional supports or tutoring that may be provided outside of school. The team should consider how the child would be functioning *as if* these mitigating factors were *not* in place.

4. If the team concludes that the child is substantially impacted by their diagnosis, they come together to develop a list of accommodations that can support the major life activities that are impacted. This list includes the setting where each accommodation takes place and who is responsible for implementing the accommodation.

5. The Section 504 plan remains in place with the team considering annually whether the plan is still necessary or if the accommodations should be changed in any way.

Suggested Accommodations

Many schools may direct families away from requesting a Section 504 plan for various reasons. Sometimes this is because they prefer to keep the number of students on a documented Section 504 low; other times is because they may feel the Section 504 plan is unnecessary if accommodations are already being implemented in the classroom by the teacher. The latter reason is often given at the elementary level where teachers are often extremely flexible and frequently do provide accommodations on an as-needed basis for students. The benefits of securing a Section 504 are that it provides some guarantees that the accommodations will follow the student to other classrooms (like music, art, and PE) and will be in place as the child moves from one grade level to another, allowing future teachers to begin the school year with the knowledge of the accommodations that assist the student. Additionally, while it is wonderful when schools are flexible and able to provide accommodations as they are needed by students, for twice-exceptional students, having accommodations documented is necessary for them to receive the accommodations when they reach high school and are preparing for the ACT, SAT, or Advanced Placement courses. If how an accommodation is implemented in the school setting is not fully documented, it is unlikely the accommodation will be approved by the organizations responsible for administering these standardized tests.

There are some common accommodations, but accommodations can also be personalized and created specific to what the child needs. If your child has a specific need and you aren't sure what the accommodation might look like, bring up the area of concern and ask the team what ideas they might have to support this area. Table 12.1 includes a list of common accommodations.

One important note about accommodations for twice-exceptional students: Some schools will recommend a 2e student drop advanced-level coursework rather than provide

Assessments and tests	Extended time to complete tests (for example, time and a half)
	Testing in a small group (to reduce anxiety)
	Having tests read aloud
Classwork and homework	Shortened assignments/show mastery by completing "most difficult first"
	Copies of full notes or partially pre-filled notes provided for lectures
	Breaking assignments into smaller parts (for example, giving one page of a packet at a time to reduce anxiety)
Emotional regulation	Steps to take when student feels emotionally dysregulated (like specified location for a break or a staff member to check in with)
	Advance notice for any unexpected changes or transitions (like a substitute teacher or shift in the day's schedule)
Communication	Frequent check-ins to provide prompting for self-advocacy
Sensory needs	Scheduled sensory breaks
	Permission to pace in specified area of classroom
	Permission to use fidgets or other manipulatives for stimming
	Exemption from school assemblies or other loud, large group events
Anxiety	Intentional placement in groups for projects (instead of asking students to self-select groups/partners)
	Request for teachers not to call on student in front of peers without advance notice or student raising their hand

TABLE 12.1 Common Section 504 accommodations

accommodations in those courses. The teachers for those courses may not be used to providing accommodations and may feel that this somehow "waters down" the course. If your child needs the challenge and has the cognitive ability to do the coursework, but simply needs accommodations to be able to show mastery of the curriculum, advocate for them to remain in the class. *Dropping advanced-level coursework is NOT an accommodation.* An accommodation removes the barrier caused by a disability. We ask stores and businesses to provide ramps to their entrances; we don't ask wheelchair users to stop using their stores.

Life beyond High School

Transitioning from high school to college, trade school, or work is a big step and sometimes paralyzing for many students. Many kids fear making the "wrong" choice, or don't know what they want for their career and future. If a student is planning to go to college, the adjustment from a school system where there is wraparound support from the staff within a single building to a typical college experience of living on campus and working with a variety of professors can be overwhelming for some twice-exceptional kids. The good news is that colleges are adapting and providing many more supports for neurodivergent students, if college feels like the right choice for them. There are other possibilities, too.

Exploring Post-High School Options

The assumed pathway for many bright kids is that they will graduate high school and go on to a four-year degree program at a university, however, it is important to take time to fully explore all the options that are available. By the time you are making choices about what to do beyond high school, your child will have a rather good idea of what works for them and what doesn't in the educational setting. In addition to the traditional four-year college path, local community colleges (which frequently have a variety of certificates and two-year programs that can help students be career-ready) can provide a stepping-stone for students to transition from the high school environment without adding the pressure of living on campus. Trade schools and apprenticeships are also options that your child may not be aware exist.

Honors Colleges

If your child is looking forward to the academic challenge of a four-year college program but is concerned about attending a large school, it may be worth considering schools that have an honors college available. Many universities offer an honors college, which serves as a "college-within-a-college." Many honors college programs have dorms specified for honors college students, providing a more studious environment and smaller group of like-minded peers that can provide a less overwhelming experience to make friends. Honors colleges also typically offer courses that are available only to students within the honors college, along with more frequent opportunities to interact with full-time faculty.

Disabilities Services at Colleges

Many students worry that as they enter college, the supports they received at the high school will be eliminated. The process for accessing supports for a disability is much different at the college level than earlier educational institutions. It is a common misunderstanding that colleges must honor an IEP or Section 504 plan. Universities utilize "letters of accommodation" (LOA) for students needing support. The process at each university is different, but most will work with students to find strategies to help students be successful. The best plan for determining how your child will be supported is to contact the potential schools and ask for information about their process: What documentation is needed, how recent does the documentation need to be, what accommodations are available, and how are they put into place?

Twice-exceptional students entering college and seeking support for their disability will need to be able to self-advocate and access services on their own. This might mean informing professors of accommodations or making appointments at the disability services offices to take tests with extended time or in an alternate environment. Talking to potential schools' disability services to request information about the specific services that are available and how students access them should be a major component of how you and your child decide about the best fit for them in higher education.

Chapter Reflection

- ♦ What types of educational settings are available to your family? Which might best be able to meet your child's needs?
- ♦ Do you feel your child's educational needs are being met? Are they challenged while also being supported? Do you feel the need to advocate for them to receive different or additional services?
- ♦ What options is your child considering for post-high school? What supports might they need when that time arrives?

Notes

1. Peters, S. J., Rambo-Hernandez, K. E., Makel, M. C., Matthews, M. S., & Plucker, J. A. (2020). Reflections on the registered report process for "Effect of local norms on racial and ethnic representation in gifted education". *AERA Open, 6*(2). doi:10.1177/2332858420919054

2. Assouline, S. G., Assouline, S. G., Colangelo, N., & M., G. M. (2015). *A nation empowered: Evidence trumps the excuses holding back America's brightest students*. Iowa City, IA: Connie Belin & Jacqueline N. Blank International Center for Gifted Education and Talent Development, University of Iowa.

3. Montgomery County Public Schools. 2015. *Twice exceptional students: A staff guidebook*. Rockville, MD: Office of Curriculum and Instruction and Office of Special Education and Student Services.

4. Pennington, M. L., Cullinan, D., & Southern, L. B. (2014). Defining autism: Variability in state education agency definitions of and evaluations for autism spectrum disorders. *Autism Research and Treatment, 2014*, 1–8. doi:10.1155/2014/327271

13

Collaborating Effectively with School

Advocating for your child at their school can be tricky; nobody wants to feel like they are coming across as "that parent." Luckily, there are ways to communicate with school professionals that can lead to a strong collaborative relationship, allowing your child to thrive.

As you begin the process of advocating for your child at the school, it is helpful to do a little bit of self-reflection. What feelings related to your own educational experience are you carrying forward with you? How do your feelings about school influence your emotions about how your child is or isn't being supported? Does your child remind you of yourself when you were young? Many of us were neurodivergent ourselves and struggled in school, either because we burnt ourselves out trying desperately to keep up or because we were unsupported and eventually gave up, internalizing negative messages about ourselves. Colin Seale discussed the trauma many students experienced in school and how it may prevent them from effectively participating in their child's educational experience on episode 80 of the podcast. "Have we considered that going to school could be like returning to the scene of a crime [for some parents]? ... You just want to do

DOI: 10.4324/9781003237532-18

better for your kids. You're like, you know what, best bet I'm not going to be involved in this."[1] Awareness of our own experiences will help us move those memories aside and clearly see what our child needs and how we can effectively advocate for it.

I'm still surprised at the number of teachers who don't know about or understand twice-exceptional learners. Teachers in gifted education programming are generally at least aware they exist, but they may lack strategies to support them. General education, special education, and other school personnel (like administrators) may not have worked with twice-exceptional kids (that they knew of) or received any training on how to support them. Just like we presume competence with our kids, we want to presume that teachers are able to support our twice-exceptional kids, but perhaps they just haven't been exposed to information about how to support twice-exceptional learners. Gentle suggestions about resources for twice-exceptional learners, like articles, books, or podcasts, can help teachers on their journey to support all learners. In addition to helping your own child, you will be helping other twice-exceptional children, too. If it feels like your child's classroom teacher isn't open to trying new things to support your child, perhaps there is another educator who can help you reach their teachers. Perhaps their gifted education teacher, a school counselor, or an administrator might be more understanding about a twice-exceptional child's needs and be able to help advocate for their needs.

It's Okay to Ask

Sometimes the one thing that kids need to self-advocate is permission to ask. So, I'm giving you the same permission. It is okay to ask the school staff for specific strategies to be used to support your child (or other strategies to be avoided). At any time during the school year, sending a quick email or requesting a short phone call or in-person conversation is not only permitted, but encouraged. As a teacher, I always wanted to hear from my students' parents because they could give me more insight into their child than I would ever gather on my own. Teachers are the expert in their content area; you are the expert on your child.

Share your expertise and let them develop ways to adjust the content for your child's specific needs.

Many teachers, especially at the elementary level, send out a questionnaire to families at the beginning of the year, requesting information about your child. *What three words would you use to describe your child? What are their interests? Do they have any food allergies?* There is usually a space asking what else you'd like the teacher to know about your child. Use this opportunity to fill them in on the things you've learned from a lifetime of loving and supporting your child. Tell them what works and what doesn't to push them beyond their comfort zone. Are there any specific strategies that are most effective when they need reassurance? If your child's teacher (or teachers) doesn't do this as a routine at the beginning of the year, don't wait until parent–teacher conferences to initiate this conversation. A note at the beginning of the year with some background into your child can give your child's teacher a head start in supporting them through the year.

Even more powerful than a letter from you is a letter directly from your child to their teacher. Starting off the beginning of the year with your child letting their teacher know what works best for them indicates to their teacher that they are taking ownership of their needs. The first time I helped a student craft a letter to her teacher at the beginning of the school year was with a rising fifth-grade student who was experiencing significant school anxiety. The beginning of the year was always terrifying for her, resulting in tears almost every morning and resistance to going to school. We worked together to come up with what she really wanted her teacher to know: she got really nervous when other kids got in trouble because she thought she was also in trouble, she was often scared to ask anyone to be her partner for group work, and she froze up if she was called on in class and wasn't ready for it. Even though this student had a Section 504 plan, this was much more personal and described in detail the situations the student found overwhelming. She was able to deliver the letter to her teacher at the Meet the Teacher Night before school began and her teacher was able to reassure her that they'd work together on those things to make sure she felt safe and comfortable in the classroom. The start of the school year was the best she'd had.

Since then, I frequently work with my clients to draft letters to their teachers prior to the beginning of the school year. We focus on a few things that they feel like their teachers really need to know and create a few specific (but reasonable) requests. When kids find that their teachers are willing to listen to them from day one, it removes the barrier of asking for help in the future. I've found this is also very useful for students who don't qualify for an IEP or Section 504 plan, but still need some additional support.

Some twice-exceptional kids are less than great at letting us know what is happening in their day-to-day school lives, so it can be hard to know how you can help them at home. There is nothing more frustrating than getting a note or phone call that your child is struggling behaviorally or academically while you believed everything at school was going smoothly. Establishing opportunities for frequent check-ins with your child's teacher not only helps you know what to expect, but it also gives the opportunity to build a welcoming relationship and collaboration with your child's teacher. Finding ways to include your child in those conversations and decisions is even more powerful because they have a voice and are preparing for more independence in the future.

It is such a balancing act to try to find the right level of how much involvement to have with your child's school. Nobody wants to be a helicopter parent, hovering over every minute of your child's life and decisions, or worse, a lawn mower parent, mowing down every obstacle that your child faces. Communicating with the school and establishing a rapport with the teachers is going to give you the peace of mind to step back and allow your child to face their successes and failures on their own. When you trust that the school is going to catch your child if they fall, you can let them walk that journey on their own.

Creating Effective Classroom Behavior Plans

One of the hills I am willing to die on is that typical classroom behavior plans are not effective for twice-exceptional kids (well, any kids, really). Whether kids are earning or losing points based on their behavior, or flipping to a different colored card, or moving their clip up and down a spectrum of colors, these types of systems rely on behavioral techniques that provide short-term compliance, at best. At least, they aren't effective in the way we want them to be. Elementary classrooms frequently use these methods more than others, although you may see variations of them at the middle school level.

Essentially, the behavioral techniques that are utilized through these systems rely on rewards and punishments to "modify" a student's behavior. Students who are naturally well-behaved don't need these systems. Kids who struggle with behavior need something different. They need to understand the behavior and why an alternative is needed, followed by a plan to implement the alternative. Behavioral systems that rely on rewards and punishments are not neurodiversity-affirming. They induce shame and fear.

There are several reasons why these systems are not neurodiversity-affirming. First, they seek to gain compliance without comprehension. This is a risk for our neurodivergent kids who may be less likely to self-advocate in the future if they are faced with a request for compliance they don't understand. If such a request comes from someone in a position of power, they believe they must go along with the request, no questions asked. The second way these systems are not neurodiversity-affirming is that many behaviors may be beyond a child's control, even if they are aware and want to improve their behavior. For example, an ADHDer who doesn't earn enough points for an extra recess because they acted impulsively and called out in class too many times doesn't learn anything. They internalize the message that they are a bad kid, because only a bad kid would continue to do something that they know they shouldn't do. Someone who believes they are a bad kid isn't going to try to improve their behavior. Finally, for our neurodivergent kids who are already very compliant but struggle with perfectionism, the fear of being called out and losing a point or flipping a card can trigger hypervigilance and anxiety they carry with them outside of the classroom.

The only benefit to these types of programs is that they provide families with a quick way to communicate about how a child is doing at school. Knowing a child had a "blue day" or a "red day" is a quick way for parents to feel that they are being made aware of their child's behavior, but really it doesn't provide much information. If your child's school or teacher is using this type of system, request that your child's progress be limited to a very specific and targeted goal, hopefully one that the child has helped to identify as something they feel would be both beneficial and achievable.

The teachers who are most effective in working to support neurodivergent kids who show problematic behaviors focus on building a relationship with the child, understanding what is behind the behaviors, and developing a strengths-based plan to help them build awareness of how to improve the skills noted. I also wrote a book for teachers of twice-exceptional learners, which may be useful to help teachers come up with strategies to support bright, neurodivergent students; it is called *Teaching Twice-Exceptional Learners in Today's Classroom*.[2]

Open Lines of Communication

It is so easy to become protective of our kids, especially when we know they are at risk of being misunderstood. When the school reaches out to you to give you feedback about your child, especially uncomfortable feedback about academic or behavioral difficulties, remember that they trying to help your child in the best way they know how. It is so easy to feel that mama-bear impulse when we get a piece of negative feedback about our child. Trust me, I've been there (like the time I fired a note back to a teacher asking pointedly what accommodations had been attempted prior to sending the note that my ADHD child needed to "focus more" and "try harder" in class). Don't feel like you have to take a backseat in your child's education or that the school has all the answers. The understanding of neurodiversity in education is changing rapidly. Every contact with the school is a chance to create an environment where your child will thrive and be understood for who they are.

Chapter Reflection

- ◆ How do you feel about your relationship with your child's school? Who is the person at the school who you can go to if you need help advocating for your child?
- ◆ How have you involved your child in their education and in the strategies used to support them in the classroom?

Notes

1. Seale, C. (2021, March 18). Equity, ADHD, and 3e [Audio blog interview]. Retrieved from https://neurodiversitypodcast.com/home/2021/3/18/episode-80-equity-adhd-and-3e
2. Kircher-Morris, E. (2021). *Teaching twice-exceptional learners in today's classroom*. Minneapolis, MN: Free Spirit Publishing.

Final Thoughts

The world is at a turning point in its understanding of neurodiversity and, as always, when there is change and upheaval, the world can feel uncertain and empowering all at once. We're moving past the time when everyone is expected to "do things the way things have always been done," and this is going to tap into potential that has gone unnoticed for far too long. You may have been one of those neurodivergent people who has survived; our children are going to be the ones who thrive. I hope this book has helped you come up with some new ideas to support your twice-exceptional child. I wish you luck on your journey.